Advanced Praise for *Dear Charlie*...

In his homage to his son Charlie, David Corvi shares insight into how men grieve. He shares the vivid details of a man's thoughts and how men process their pain. In his letters to his son, he provides an awareness of how the loss of a child born sleeping is different than many other losses. His navigation from the excitement of expectation to the unfathomable darkness of disappointment shows the emotion men experience. David's words are revelatory, healing, and inspirational, helping other men to find their way again after child loss.

—Dr. Michael Bullock
President, Mile's Mission

Dear Charlie...Letters to My Son by David Corvi is a profoundly moving and beautifully written collection that navigates the depths of grief and the enduring power of love. Through a series of heartfelt letters penned in the year following his son Charlie's stillbirth, David invites readers into the raw and intimate journey of a father's sorrow and loss. This book is not just a testament to the unique bond between father and child but also a poignant reminder of the shared human experience of loss and remembrance. David's words resonate with honesty and vulnerability, making "Dear Charlie" a must-read for anyone touched by the pain of losing a loved one.

—Missy Thomas
Executive Director, Now I Lay Me Down To Sleep

David's letters to his cherished son Charlie are truly filled with pure love. The shock of his beloved son's death is raw as David shares the devastation and complexities of the suddenness, yet his love runs through every word, missing his baby and the dreams shared by him and his wife Katherine.

Discovering, too, this Love is too big, beautiful, and lasting to ever be "gone." Knowing there are others suffering from child loss, David's confusion and growing awareness are carried with his deep love and a gentleness that if he can help others on their complex journeys, his grief shared through Dear Charlie will be a source of healing for others as well. In the ways David and I and others on our committee reach out to grieving parents and families through our Angel of Hope Children's Memorial in Stow, Ohio, we have learned that as we come together in that oneness of grief and love, we are not nearly as alone as we once thought. And our love expands…

—Sara Ruble
Grief and Healing Facilitator
Angel of Hope Children's Memorial, Stow, Ohio

The anticipation of fatherhood fills itself with joy, laughter, hope, honor, and pride, a chance to build a legacy. However, prepare yourself as David takes us on an unexpected journey of grief, pain, vulnerability, strength, and courage as he reveals a father's greatest loss, that of his precious son. Dear Charlie helps us to navigate a narrative of togetherness with communities both familiar and new. Prepare to embrace the innermost thoughts and feelings of a father's quest to find peace by turning sorrow into healing. A great read for every parent, especially fathers who are seeking emotional sanctuary.

—Tammie S. Jones, MS
Senior Director of Programs & Behavioral Health,
Birthing Beautiful Communities

We are a part of the bereaved family community, and *Dear Charlie…* gives a perspective on grief that is not only vulnerable but very accurate in giving a glimpse on what goes through the thoughts of a parent grieving after the loss of a child. The heaviness of such a loss can be felt with each word, and we believe *Dear Charlie...* will speak to other families on their own journey.

—Katie Benden and Sarah Ernst
Maryland Chapter Co-Leaders,
Reflections Grief and Wellness Care

It is a rare find to read the inner thoughts of a man grieving related to pregnancy/infant loss. Our society often gives men the impression that they are supposed to "be the rock" for the family and push their grief away to support others. *Dear Charlie...* is a welcome, heartfelt book of letters, giving men permission to grieve, feel, and process the heavy emotions and thoughts that come with coping with the death of a child. This book fills a gaping hole in pregnancy loss books: the male perspective.

—Jessica Correnti
Author of *The ABCs of Grief* and Certified Child Life
Specialist, Kids Grief Support

A book about grief from the perspective of a father is unique on its own; however, sharing heartfelt emotions and thoughts in the form of letters to his son is even more unique. These letters from the heart tell a story that needs to be shared—a story that is experienced by many parents. The letters in *Dear Charlie...* will relate to the hearts and pain of many and hopefully help people feel a little less alone in their grief.

—Amy Tatz
President, Back In His Arms Again

Like a fishing line cast into the murky depths of his persistent, if unwelcome grief, each letter David shares with us creates a tenuous bridge, reeling in memories and weaving new connections to his beloved infant son, keeping Charlie's spirit alive in a profound and tender way. On reading it, I felt like I was sitting on the dock with the two of them, a silent witness to the incredible, real, and lasting bond between a father and his son.

For anyone navigating the loss of a child, *Dear Charlie...* will no doubt be a comforting companion on that journey.

—Mary McKenna
Community & Donor Engagement Manager,
Hudson Community Foundation

What a beautiful and brilliant way David chose to stay connected to Charlie. I read *Dear Charlie...* with tears in my eyes and a smile on my face. It is a beacon of love from a father to his son, whom he misses dearly. Equal parts heartbreaking and heartwarming, these letters offer genuine insight through the lens of a loss dad. As a fellow loss parent, you'll gain immense validation through reading these letters. As the loved one of a loss parent, you'll gain immense perspective through reading these letters. Love and longing often coexist, and *Dear Charlie...* articulates that gorgeously.

—Rob Reider
Co-Founder and Executive Director,
SAD DADS CLUB

DEAR CHARLIE...
LETTERS TO MY SON

A FATHER'S JOURNEY OF LOSS, GRIEF, AND REMEMBRANCE

DEAR CHARLIE...
LETTERS TO MY SON

A FATHER'S JOURNEY OF LOSS, GRIEF, AND REMEMBRANCE

DAVID CORVI

ethos
collective

Dear Charlie... © 2024 by David Corvi. All rights reserved.

Printed in the United States of America

Published by Igniting Souls
PO Box 43, Powell, OH 43065
IgnitingSouls.com

This book contains material protected under international and federal copyright laws and treaties. Any unauthorized reprint or use of this material is prohibited. No part of this book may be reproduced or transmitted in any form or by any means, electronic or mechanical, including photocopying, recording, or by any information storage and retrieval system, without express written permission from the author.

LCCN: 2024911056
Paperback ISBN: 978-1-63680-307-4
Hardcover ISBN: 978-1-63680-308-1
e-book ISBN: 978-1-63680-309-8

Available in paperback, hardcover, e-book, and audiobook.

Scripture texts in this work are taken from the New American Bible, revised edition© 2010, 1991, 1986, 1970 Confraternity of Christian Doctrine, Washington, D.C. and are used by permission of the copyright owner. All Rights Reserved. No part of the New American Bible may be reproduced in any form without permission in writing from the copyright owner.

Any Internet addresses (websites, blogs, etc.) and telephone numbers printed in this book are offered as a resource. They are not intended in any way to be or imply an endorsement by Igniting Souls, nor does Igniting Souls vouch for the content of these sites and numbers for the life of this book.

Some names and identifying details may have been changed to protect the privacy of individuals.

This book is dedicated to all parents
who've experienced the loss of a child
and all our babies gone too soon.

Table of Contents

Acknowledgments xiii
Dear Reader xv
Introduction xvii
Letter 1 - December 15, 2021 1
Letter 2 - January 1, 2022 10
Letter 3 - January 15, 2022 14
Letter 4 - February 1, 2022 23
Letter 5 - February 26, 2022 29
Letter 6 - March 11, 2022 34
Letter 7 - March 24, 2022 41
Letter 8 - April 13, 2022 46
Letter 9 - May 12, 2022 50
Letter 10 - May 17, 2022 55
Letter 11 - June 23, 2022 62
Letter 12 - July 7, 2022 66
Letter 13 - August 6, 2022 71
Letter 14 - September 6, 2022 76

Letter 15 - September 25, 2022 81
Letter 16 - October 26, 2022 87
Letter 17 - December 6, 2022 93
Letter 18 - May 27, 2024 96
Recommended Readings 103
Resources 105

Acknowledgments

Writing this book has been an emotional journey, and it would not have been possible without the support and encouragement of many wonderful people.

First and foremost, I want to thank Charlie. Your impact on our lives is immeasurable. This book is for you, my sweet boy.

To my wife, Katherine, and our children, William, Alexander, and Louis. Thank you for your endless love and support. Your presence has been a beacon of light during the darkest of times.

To Katherine and Charlie's medical team, especially her primary OB-GYN, Dr. Dinkar Rao. Thank you for your incredible compassion and care in supporting us during this tragedy.

Father Cyril Pinchak, thank you for baptizing Charlie and officiating his funeral. Your unconditional friendship and spiritual guidance have been invaluable.

To Don Ferfoglia and Ferfoglia Funeral Homes, thank you for organizing Charlie's wake and funeral and taking care

Acknowledgments

of him after leaving the hospital. Your care and professionalism brought comfort during a very difficult time.

To my siblings, your unwavering support has been a source of strength. Thank you for standing by my family through this journey.

Amy Jordan and the Hudson Community Foundation, thank you for managing Charlie's Fund and ensuring that Charlie's legacy continues to make a positive impact. To everyone who has donated to and supported Charlie's Fund and participated in his Challenges, your generosity and compassion are deeply appreciated.

To my parents, your love and support have been a constant comfort. Thank you for being there for our family and for helping us navigate this difficult path.

To Bob Proehl, who read an early version of my letters to Charlie. Your initial read-through and feedback around aboutness were invaluable.

To Michael Bullock who connected me with Igniting Souls. Charlie and Miles were definitely looking after us the day we met.

To my cousin, Ali Bonomo, for designing Charlie's website and the cover of this book. You're one of my favorite people.

Travis White, my project manager, thank you for your guidance and for keeping this project on track. Your dedication and compassion have been invaluable.

Micaela Eberly, my editor, your keen eye and thoughtful feedback have helped shape Charlie's letters. Thank you for your insights and expertise.

Finally, to all the friends, family, and strangers who offered their support and shared in our grief, your kindness has been a source of solace and strength.

Thank you all from the bottom of my heart.

Dear Reader

Our son, Charles Martin Corvi, was stillborn on October 26, 2021. He was 15 days shy of his due date.

Charlie is not here to tell his own story, so we must do it for him.

This is Charlie's story.

Dear Charlie... is a series of letters I wrote to my third son. Talking to him has helped keep him close to my heart and supported me through my own grief. The letters serve as a record of this traumatizing event for our family, a celebration of all he is to us and our world, and the journey through my own grief.

Men grieve differently than women. There is no right or wrong way; it is just different. I grieve by doing, which helps me try to make sense of this awful tragedy that occurred. Will I ever find an answer? Probably not. This is how I process my grief and the loss, both of which are a part of me now.

Disclaimer: The emotions and thoughts I describe in these letters are my own. They are the raw emotions and real thoughts of a father grieving the death of his child. They are not intended to offend, criticize, or blame. If that happens, I apologize in advance.

The letters were written in real-time during the year after Charlie died. They conclude on his first birthday. This is not to illustrate that grief follows a timeline and is finite. It doesn't and is not. People will experience varying lengths and depths of emotions at different times. I've learned many things from Charlie—most notably, that grief is never-ending. It rolls over our family like the coming and going of the tide. Day in, day out. Week in, week out. Some days, it comes crashing down on us with tremendous force. On other days, it ripples softly over us. It's been more than two years since Charlie died, and I still experience whirlwinds of emotions that change before I can get used to them. I've met parents who are decades into the journey of loss and grief, and their anger and disbelief are palpable.

You will notice multiple emotions weaving through each letter. A letter may start with anger and frustration, touch on disbelief and denial, and conclude with what feels like gratitude. This is completely normal, too. Grief is messy and complex. Charlie has taught us two things can be true. We can miss him and be sad while also celebrating the incredible impact he has on our family and others who've experienced pregnancy or infant loss.

Lastly, the biggest comfort and support through our grief has been the opportunity to connect with others who have experienced the similar loss of a child—a greater number than there ever should be. I hope sharing Charlie's story will help others on their own path of loss, grief, remembrance, and healing. You are not alone.

David Corvi

Introduction

Parenting after loss is challenging. Mothering is not just about meeting our children's needs; it's about meeting our needs so we are able to give them what they need. I've found communicating openly and honestly with my partner, spending time with my living children, and honoring and parenting my Charlie to be most helpful for me on this journey. I read, and I journal, and I seek therapy. Stillbirth has forever changed me as a mother. I don't take for granted their breaths, heartbeats, laughs, or cries. Hold them, hear them, love them, see them, and allow them to do the same with you.

Fathers grieve, too. My David fixes problems. He protects us. He couldn't fix or protect Charlie, and that made no sense to him. As a result, he felt and continues to feel anger and sadness. He was devastated to see and hear my physical and emotional pain after delivering our son. He continues to cope by taking care of our boys and me, training for a marathon, joining a local children's memorial, constructing a cedar chest for all Charlie's belongings, and starting a fund in his memory.

Introduction

He also writes letters to Charlie, and when he reads them to me, he parents Charlie in a way that we will never otherwise have the chance to.

These are his letters to Charlie.

Katherine Corvi
May 2022

Letter 1

> Grief is not a disorder, a disease, or a sign of weakness. It is an emotional, physical, and spiritual necessity, the price you pay for love. The only cure for grief is to grieve.
>
> —Earl Grollman

December 15, 2021

Dear Charlie,

    I'm sorry for not writing to you sooner. I started writing letters to your oldest brother, William, intending to share advice and express the depth of your mother's and my love. The tradition continued with Alexander when he was born. Your mother asked if I planned to write to you, and each time, I faltered. The weight of your absence was too heavy, too raw. It's been seven long weeks since our world shattered, and you slipped away. Seven weeks of grappling with the gaping hole you've left behind.

    Christmas looms just two weeks away. In an alternate world, you'd be a month old, lying next to a stuffed giraffe from Mema with a little 1-month sticker proudly displayed on your shirt. Today, your Christmas stocking arrived, triggering

Letter 1

the words that have evaded me. The boys were overjoyed to hang it by the fireplace as if making space for you among us. Their pride in being big brothers is both touching and bittersweet.

It's surreal that more than a month has gone by since you left us. There are moments when it feels like this nightmare never unfolded like it's a sick, twisted dream. In those moments, I question if I truly felt your kicks in your mother's belly, if I genuinely heard the rhythm of your heartbeat in the doctor's office. It's hard to believe you're gone. The joy of waiting for you has been replaced by the sad truth that you're not here. The boys' excitement to meet their little brother, the anticipation of your presence, all resemble fragments of a reality that was never truly ours.

I write this letter with a heavy heart, trying to make sense of the profound loss we've experienced. Your absence has left a permanent mark on our lives, and I find solace in this letter as a means to connect with you, even across the boundaries that separate our worlds. The disbelief that such a vibrant presence could vanish, the attempts to minimize the overwhelming pain by pretending the loss hasn't occurred—these are the defense mechanisms we employ to navigate our journey of grief.

Your mother and I endlessly replay the events of that day:

She woke about 5 a.m. to your kicks that Monday morning. Were they your last? That was the last time she felt you. She had taken a personal day from work since your brothers were both off school for the holiday. It was a crisp autumn day in late October. Northeast Ohio is purely splendid on days like those. We planned a family hike in the Cuyahoga Valley National Park. Your mother was 37 weeks and 6 days pregnant.

Videos we captured from that weekend show the boys cutting dinosaurs out of pink construction paper, dancing with mom in our kitchen, scrambling rock faces in the national park, and shuffling our feet over the leaf-filled trails.

The video not captured is the one etched in our minds forever:

After our hike, we decided to have a lazy day at home. The boys wanted to feel you in Mom's belly, so they all snuggled up on the living room floor. I went to the garage to work on a carpentry project I had recently started—a shelf for my record player. After a while, your mother opened the door and stepped out to the landing.

"We're not feeling the baby," she said. "If this little guy doesn't move in the next hour, I'm going to the hospital. I'll drink some cold water and lie down upstairs to see if I can get him to move. Can you keep an eye on the boys?"

You see, Charlie, one of the things your mother loves about me is my ability to remain calm and level-headed during some of the most unpredictable and uncertain circumstances. Call it naivety or my personal disposition, but I tend not to overreact to situations. My response to your mother was no different. I said OK and went inside to play with your brothers. It wasn't abnormal that she didn't feel you. You were usually calm in her belly, much like your brother, Alexander. She just felt your kicks that morning, so I didn't think much of it.

Thirty minutes later, however, your mother was standing at the door with bags in her hand. She was putting on her coat. "He hasn't moved. I called my OB. He said to go to L&D; he'll meet me there. I'm driving to the hospital." What didn't register before did now. I could see the fear and worry in her eyes. She had gone pale. She was frantic. I remained calm.

"Wait," I said. "I need to go with you. What if they keep you there? What if you have to deliver? I'll call Jeff, and we can drop off the boys." Solving problems. Fixing things. That's what I'm good at. Little did I know at the time, I couldn't fix this.

Letter 1

We scrambled to get the boys in the car and dropped them off at my cousin's house in the next neighborhood. We then drove the 25 minutes, what felt like an eternity, to our hospital. Your mother knew something was very wrong, and she thought you might have died. I kept telling her let's wait and see; let's wait and see. We both hoped she was wrong. But a mother knows.

The connection a mother has to her child is something a father will never comprehend. Sure, we have a connection to our children, and I love you and your brothers more than any words can ever explain. But a mother is connected to her child at a much more intimate level, a level of carrying her baby inside her for 40 weeks. Of knowing the feeling of *her* baby, a feeling no one else will ever know or experience. She said you were sitting differently in her belly, not like before. Men can never understand a mother's connection to her child. But a mother knows.

Our minds are a unique organ. In times of joy and exhilaration, they speed things up. In times of pain and worry, they slow things down. I can remember almost every detail of that day—the slow, quiet walk down the long hallway to Labor and Delivery. We left the car on the second floor of the parking garage. The nurse who checked us in was scripted and aloof, void of any sense of urgency. "I'm sure it's nothing. I'm not really sure which doctor is on right now," she said, looking around as if a doctor would magically appear. "But just have a seat, and I'll go check for you." Why did we need to know all this information? Was there a doctor on the floor or not? She wasn't doing anything to calm us down. Instead, she downplayed our fear, acting as if we had no reason to worry. She was making it worse. We didn't sit.

After several long minutes, we were placed in Triage Room 4. It was small and cramped, with the ultrasound machine on one side of the bed and the door to the bathroom on the other. The walls were white and sterile. I leaned against the window, which overlooked the rooftop of the building next door. The fans of the AC units were spinning. Your mother's OB rushed into the room, out of breath. His feet, like always, were stuffed haphazardly into his sneakers; the back collars of them flattened. "Do you mind if I take off my mask? I ran from the other side of the hospital." He's a small, elderly Indian man with, as we would come to know him better, overflowing compassion and a heart the size of a mountain.

A short while later, we were surrounded by his medical team, staring at the familiar image of your heart on the ultrasound machine. The only noise in the room was the hollow vibration of the microphone on your mother's belly. The silence in the hospital room bore an unbearable weight. Everyone held their breath, desperate to hear the echo of your heartbeat. The resident physician's voice was steady. She was telling us something, "I want to show you what I see."

Your heart had stopped beating.

My head was spinning. Questions tormented me: Stopped? Stopped? What does that mean? Was the equipment faulty? Were they using it correctly? Were we looking at the right thing? In a place designed to preserve life, why was no one moving to save you? "Nothing could be done," they claimed. "The definition of an accident."

I didn't believe them. I still don't. With all our advances in medical practices, how could they not see what was happening to you? How could they remain oblivious? We were thrust into shock, and the grip of disbelief still hasn't loosened. In my desperate attempt to make sense of the senseless, I tell your mother you were so eager to meet your older brothers that you got all tangled up. It's a fragile comfort, if only for a fleeting moment. In a twist, your mother was the calm one and the person who touched my arm softly and told me there was nothing else that could be done.

Letter 1

Your mother. She's an incredible woman. I used to joke about her being the toughest person I know. Your brothers' arrivals were natural, spontaneous, without any medical interventions. What she endured that day to bring you to us, and what she continues to endure. All without you. It's a journey I'm still grappling to comprehend. And yet, every morning, she rises, navigates through the routines of the day, showers, sees your brothers off to school, and engages with a world you'll never know. As a pediatric psychologist, she cares for her patients, facing the cruel irony of assisting others who may share a similar experience and bear the weight of a loss she knows too well. Now, it's an undeniable fact that she is the strongest person in my world.

We try to find solace in knowing you were surrounded by your mother and brothers when you passed. That Monday, all four of you laid on the floor, a tight-knit huddle. The boys pressed their hands and ears against your mother's belly, eager to feel your movements. Joy slowly morphed into fear as they struggled to feel you. You were so close to being with us.

For me, the most agonizing part of the day is dinner. The dining room resonates with an eerie quietness, the table appearing vast and empty. In the days before your mother carried you in her womb when there were only four of us, I used to tell her it felt like someone was missing. Now, the reality is stark—someone *is* missing. Missing from the anticipated joys and wonders your childhood would unfold, first sounds, steps, laughs, words. You'll miss the simple pleasures of each season: bright flowers, the warm sun, cool wind, bitter snow.

You'll miss the warmth of baths, the comfort of bedtime stories, and the exhilaration of jumping into piles of leaves. You'll never experience wrestling in the basement with your brothers and me, the laughter with friends and cousins, the love from grandparents. The unfairness of it all is overwhelming.

While I started these letters to William and Alexander to share advice, now it's you I turn to for guidance and strength. In your absence, I've already learned so much, like how to love more deeply, how to navigate the complexity of grief, how to unveil emotions hidden too long, and how to embrace the present. Thank you for being our silent teacher, for making the ultimate sacrifice to watch over us. You've altered our lives in ways beyond our grasp, and for that, we are eternally grateful.

Wherever you are and whatever you are doing, Charlie, know you are loved and missed more than words can express.

Love,
Dad

Letter 1

Holding Charlie, Now I Lay Me Down to Sleep, Marti Wagner

Katherine with Charlie, Now I Lay Me Down To Sleep, Marti Wagner

Charlie's Stocking, Christmas 2021

Charlie's Stocking on our mantle, Christmas 2021

Letter 2

I will not say: Do not weep; for not all tears are an evil.

—J.R.R. Tolkien

January 1, 2022

Dear Charlie,

Today marks the first day of the new year. It's been over two months since you left us, and as we navigate the many firsts without you, the disbelief lingers like an unwelcome shadow. This year's family photos hang on the wall of the living room. They are a stark reminder of your absence. You should have been in the photos. Even though we took them a few short weeks ago, Mom shows no signs of being pregnant. It's as if she never was—as if you were never in her belly.

Christmas, once a season of enchantment, came and went, leaving a void that echoed through every moment, constantly reminding us of your absence. The annual tradition of cutting down a tree, a task once filled with anticipation and joy, was shrouded in a surreal fog this year. As we trudged through the snow-covered fields, the crisp winter air should have been accompanied by your smiles, your tiny hands reaching out to touch the world around you. Yet, reality struck hard. The lack of your presence was palpable in the quiet rustle of evergreen branches.

Decorating the tree became a bittersweet affair. Each ornament, once a symbol of happiness and family unity, now bore the weight of an unimaginable loss. The lights that adorned the branches cast a somber glow as if mourning the laughter and delight that should have filled the room. Your presence was felt in the haunting echoes of what should have been.

The songs playing on the radio carried a different tune this year. Each note seemed to harmonize with the ache in our hearts, a melody of grief and disbelief that drowned out the festive spirit. The twinkling lights clinging to the houses mocked the darkness that had settled within us. The world outside continued its revelry, oblivious to the shattered reality within our walls.

Christmas morning arrived with an emptiness that even the excitement of unwrapping presents couldn't fill. The boys, in their innocent enthusiasm, tore through wrapping paper, their laughter reverberating through the house. But in those moments, the void widened, your absence magnified by the joyful chaos that should have included you. "Charlie would be here with us," we repeated, a mantra to bridge the gap between what is and what should have been.

The emotions we've grappled with defy the simplicity of singular feelings. Your mother, a vessel of deep emotions, articulated it first. She feels with her entire being, a blessing and a burden. Until now, life allowed us to experience one emotion at a time. Birthdays meant happiness; celebrations meant joy. Now, emotions blend together in a complex tapestry woven with threads of joy, sorrow, frustration, and anger.

The boys have become unwitting conduits of this emotional symphony. William, the ever-thoughtful big brother, leaves tokens of affection next to your urn as tangible

Letter 2

reminders of the void you've left. Alexander, in his innocent wisdom, speaks of the day when you will come out of your "box" and love Mommy. The juxtaposition of their love and innocence with the harsh reality is both heartwarming and heart-wrenching.

In these moments, emotions collide, a chaotic mix of happiness and sadness, joy and frustration, love and anger. The contradictions are striking: happiness that the boys embrace you as their brother, sadness that you're not physically present, frustration that you miss being part of their lives, and rage at the unfairness of it all.

This roller coaster of emotions has become our new reality. Feeling the warmth of family, the laughter of William and Alexander, the embrace of your mother, and then, in the same breath, grappling with the sorrow and fury of our loss. The waves of emotion are relentless, crashing over us with a force we never knew existed.

I began writing these letters with the intention of offering advice or reflections to William and Alexander. Little did I know the lessons would be reciprocal. You've taught us how to navigate this sea of emotions, to laugh in joy, cry in sorrow, and scream in anger—all at the same time. Thank you for this wisdom and for the grace to ride these turbulent waves.

Wherever you are and whatever you're doing, please know your mother and I love you more than anything.

Love,
Dad

Charlie's urn with little trinkets left by his brothers

Letter 3

Blessed are those who mourn,
for they will be comforted.

—Matthew 5:4

January 15, 2022

Dear Charlie,

    Growing up, the bond with my brother Ernie was unparalleled. He's only 15 months older than me, and it feels like we've been side by side since the beginning of time. We practically lived in each other's pockets, sharing a bedroom for 13 years. From sports to summer camps, we did everything together, and our friends often mistook us for twins.

    Ernie found his match in your Aunt Andrea, his high school sweetheart. Their love story spans over two decades, and has blossomed into a beautiful family of five. Andrea's twin brother, Cyril, added another layer to our close-knit circle. Cyril was a sports enthusiast like us, excelling in varsity hockey and track during our high school days at Gilmour Academy in Gates Mills, Ohio.

I still remember my "shadow day" at Gilmour in eighth grade, where incoming students like me got a taste of what the school had to offer. Cyril, being a student ambassador, was assigned to be my guide.

After completing college, Cyril pursued a path of spiritual devotion, entering the seminary to become a Jesuit priest. Second only to the medical team, Cyril was among the first to arrive at the hospital the morning we lost you. The night of your passing, I reached out to Ernie for support. His immediate response was to call Cyril. "He'll baptize Charlie," he assured me.

It's funny how life comes full circle, isn't it?

Cyril arrived promptly at 7 a.m. on October 26th. Despite the passing years, he hadn't lost his gentle demeanor. His comforting presence filled our hospital room as he greeted us with familiar warmth. When offered the chance to hold you, he accepted graciously, cradling your delicate body in his sturdy hands. As he held you close, Cyril offered prayers and bestowed a blessing upon you. Then, with genuine concern, he inquired about our well-being.

In the ensuing conversation, I couldn't conceal the turmoil of disbelief and anger brewing within me. Like many men faced with such a tragedy, my initial instinct was to find a solution, to uncover what went awry and why it couldn't have been prevented. Failing to rectify the situation, my focus shifted to shielding your mother and our family from further pain. My plan was straightforward: avoid discussing the events altogether. Opting for a modest funeral, we'd confide our grief solely with family, eschewing any grand gestures. We'd choose cremation, keeping you close, and I'd assume the responsibility of caring for your mother at home.

In essence, I longed to return to the semblance of our former life.

As Cyril cradled you in his arms, his presence exuded familiarity and understanding. Having known me for years,

Letter 3

he had witnessed my fervor during high school athletic events and observed my devotion to family during holiday gatherings. With characteristic gentleness, he lightly challenged my inclination to retreat into normalcy.

"It's only natural to want to shut everyone out, to hurriedly seal off this chapter and return to the life we once knew," Cyril remarked softly. "But I believe this urge stems from the darkness, from forces seeking to isolate you. You've experienced a profound tragedy, yet we are beings wired for connection. Don't shut yourself off. Allow others to enter your world. Let them help you."

From that pivotal moment, I felt a surge of determination to share your story with the world. I spent the remainder of the day reaching out to friends and family, spurred by Cyril's counsel. Embracing his advice to open up and accept assistance, I was overwhelmed by the outpouring of love and support from those who reached out. Their kindness provided solace amid the darkness.

Additionally, I felt compelled to ensure that everyone knew the truth of what had transpired. I feared the potential anguish your mother might endure months later should she encounter someone unaware of our loss. The thought of her having to recount your passing, reopening the wounds of our grief, filled me with dread. If I couldn't undo the tragedy that befell you, at least I could shield your mother from further pain.

We devoted the entire day to you, cherishing every moment we could spend holding you close. Cyril performed your baptism, bringing a sense of solemnity to the hospital room. When my mother arrived, she cradled you in her arms, unwilling to let go. Then came Uncle Ernie, his unexpected presence a source of comfort. I'll never forget the overwhelming surge of emotion when I found him standing in the hallway of the hospital, having driven four hours across the state just to be with us. He hugged me, and I cried uncontrollably for a few minutes. His support meant everything to me at that moment.

We're grateful for the precious moments we shared with you. The hospital provided a cuddle cot, a tender gesture ensuring you remained by our side. Nurses and Child Life Specialists visited our room, crafting memory boxes filled with keepsakes: your handprints, footprints, measurements, and photographs. Later that day, my sisters Erica and Kristen, along with my dad, gathered at our house, offering their unconditional support. Mema, your mom's mom, made the journey from New York the following day, further strengthening our familial bonds during this time of sorrow.

As evening approached, the inevitability of saying goodbye weighed heavy on our hearts. The cuddle cot, though comforting, couldn't halt the inevitable decline of your fragile form. The funeral home dispatched two gentlemen to transport you from the hospital, marking the final time we would hold you in our arms. With tears streaming down our faces, we gently placed you in a white satin-lined rectangular box provided by the funeral home. The drive home felt long and somber, each mile laden with the weight of our grief. We stopped to refuel the car, a routine task amid the overwhelming grief we were experiencing.

The following day, we made our way straight to the funeral home to make arrangements. Ferfoglia Funeral Home stood tall—a grand red brick colonial-style building nestled south of Route 82 in Macedonia. Upon our arrival, a receptionist greeted us warmly and led us to a small conference room. An accent table with a Keurig machine caught my eye, its neatly arranged cups, creamers, sugar, and pods offering a surreal contrast to the somber occasion.

As we settled in, Don, the funeral home patriarch, joined us, gently navigating through the details of your funeral arrangements—the location, the choice of casket, the arrangements for cremation, and the selection of an urn. Despite

Letter 3

his compassionate demeanor, disbelief lingered in my mind. Throughout the discussion, I clung tightly to your mother's hand, seeking comfort in her presence. As Don momentarily stepped out, I couldn't help but voice my disbelief. "This kind of thing doesn't happen to us," I muttered, struggling to come to terms with our new reality. "What the hell are we doing here?" In grief, denial can manifest as a defense mechanism, shielding us from the overwhelming pain of loss by rejecting the truth of the situation.

Your funeral was held at Our Lady Chapel on the campus of Gilmour Academy on Saturday, October 30th. Cyril presided over the mass. Nearly 200 people attended, including family, friends, colleagues, and the students and parents of the entire Gilmour varsity soccer team, who I coached. Your aunts and uncles served as pallbearers. Aunt Kristen cried the entire walk down the center aisle. We sat in the very front row. Your tiny casket was to our immediate left. I had attended mass almost every Sunday for as long as I could remember. I could recite the entirety of it in my sleep. As the service progressed, the melodic rituals of the Catholic mass did little to comfort my grief. The sequence of prayers and readings—Opening prayer, First Reading, Responsorial Psalm, Second Reading, Gospel Acclamation, Gospel, Homily, Profession of Faith, Communion, and Universal Prayer—seemed to blur together as I grappled with the pain and anguish of losing you. Despite my efforts to maintain composure for your mom and brothers, the sight of your marble-white casket in my periphery overshadowed everything else.

Cyril's voice resonated through the chapel as he delivered the homily. As I realized we had already progressed through 20 minutes of the service, I found myself taking a few deep breaths. Cyril's presence at your funeral provided a momentary respite from my pain, allowing me to focus intently on his words.

"Why is it that sin and evil exist? I don't have an answer. Why is it that Charles Martin had to die? I don't have an answer. It's an impossible task to try to explain it,"

Cyril's voice echoed with solemnity. His words struck a chord within me, acknowledging the incomprehensible nature of our loss.

"No one is demanding that you do well with this. Even God is not demanding that you do well with this. No one is demanding that you give up your hurt and your anger . . . don't be too quick to judge your anger, your righteous anger. You have every right to be upset,"

Cyril continued, his words offering support amid the turmoil of emotions.

"Charles had nothing but love and knew nothing but love."

Recalling his words from the day of your birth, Cyril reiterated,

"The devil is going to try to alienate you, to fragment you, to keep you apart from the people who love you and care for you in this time of need. Don't let that temptation win. Everyone present here is grieving too, and evil, by its nature, wants to fragment us, wants to alienate us, to drive us alone away from God and away from each other . . . and so, we have to stay together. We can't let the devil drive us apart. We can't let evil fragment us even further. . . . David and Katherine, you were talking about how you questioned, 'Why did we move to Cleveland in the middle of the pandemic?' You talked about the struggle of not having a community and wanting some community for your children. And then you said a beautiful thing, 'The gift of the

Letter 3

funeral tomorrow will be the answer to the question, who is our community?' Take a moment. Look around and see your community."

I couldn't bring myself to turn around. The thought of meeting everyone's gaze filled me with apprehension. Instead, I focused on the varsity soccer players and offered them a wave. They felt like a sanctuary—a group that knew me more as a coach than personally. With them, I could maintain the façade of composure. After all, I had spent years on the field, where men are expected to be tough.

Meanwhile, my friends, aunts, uncles, cousins, nieces, nephews, siblings, and parents were seated behind me. They knew me intimately, having witnessed my journey from youth to fatherhood. They understood the emotional turmoil lurking beneath my stoic exterior. Avoiding their gaze was necessary; meeting their eyes threatened to unravel my composure, and I needed to remain strong for your mother.

In that moment, your mother's touch grounded me. Sensing my inner turmoil, she silently conveyed her support, nodding toward the rows behind us. Tears welled in my eyes as she squeezed my hand tighter, a wordless reassurance that she was by my side. Glancing over my shoulder, I saw row after row of family and friends, some 200 strong, gathered to honor you and offer their support. The sheer magnitude of their presence overwhelmed me. Unable to hold anyone's gaze, I averted my eyes, scanning over the heads of the assembled crowd, too afraid to make direct eye contact.

As Cyril continued to speak, I found myself pondering the significance of his presence in our lives. Was it mere coincidence, or was it destined from the moment I shadowed him in high school? Did fate intertwine our paths, leading him to be a part of our family's saddest moments—the day you died, your baptism, and now, your funeral?

Reflecting on the group of people who gathered to support us, I felt a profound sense of gratitude. Moving to Cleveland from Philadelphia just a year ago had left us feeling adrift, searching for a sense of belonging and community in our new surroundings. Little did we know the individuals gathered at your funeral would become our newfound community—their unwavering support providing relief in our darkest hour.

Thank you, Charlie, for the invaluable gift of these connections. In the aftermath of your birth, we've forged bonds within our community that run deeper than we ever imagined possible.

Wherever you may be, know your mother, and I love you very, very much.

Love,
Dad

Letter 3

Father Cyril Pinchak speaking during Charlie's funeral; Gilmour soccer team in the upper left corner

Our Lady Chapel at Gilmour Academy during Charlie's funeral

Letter 4

Grief is the last act of love we have to give to those we loved. Where there is deep grief, there was great love.

—Unknown

February 1, 2022

Dear Charlie,

I wear a beard. It's become a signature of sorts, a facial garment I've had on and off for about 15 years. I sprouted it in the early days of my teaching career, thinking it might lend a touch of maturity to my fresh-faced appearance in front of high school students. Your grandfather, with his persistent questions about shaving, and Uncle Ernie, who humorously remarked on my "bearded phase on display" during his best man speech at my wedding, have been keen observers of this facial hair journey.

These days, the beard garners even more attention as it grows longer and thicker. People comment, some in jest, others genuinely curious, "Nice beard" or "Your beard is getting long." "It's Charlie's Beard," I tell them, launching into the tale that links the growth and shearing of these whiskers

Letter 4

to the births of your brothers and the unique connection it symbolizes.

When William was born, I shaved off the beard I had nurtured for years. I made a short trip home from the hospital to shower and change clothes. Looking at my reflection in the mirror, I made a split decision. It was a momentary impulse driven by the desire for William to feel the smoothness of my face against his tiny cheek. When I returned to the hospital, your mother, briefly taken aback by my sudden change in appearance, soon understood the sentiment. Fast forward two and a half years to Alexander's birth, and history repeated itself. The beard came off again, carrying the weight of tradition and a silent promise to each new addition to our family.

And then came you, my sweet Charlie. Before the funeral, five days after your birth, at a time when shaving was the furthest thing from my mind, I noticed the beard had lingered. The tradition of removing my facial hair for you to feel my smooth skin had completely escaped me. I stared at the red eyes and hollow appearance of the face in the mirror. They were worn down from sleepless and tear-filled nights. I couldn't muster the strength to let the beard go. It meant letting *you* go. In the months that followed, the beard became more than just facial hair; it was a testament to loss, a refusal to let go of something I held dear. You.

I'm unloading this agony onto you now because I realize you'll never get to know the contours of my face–the hazel eyes, the light brown hair, the slightly crooked nose, or the small gap between my front teeth. One of the best experiences as a parent is standing at the classroom door of your child's daycare, and in a slow second, when their eyes meet yours, your face becomes recognizable to them. So much joy is contained in that one moment in time.

You and I will never share that moment.

I also realize you won't get to know your mother's features either—her captivating green eyes, her long, thin, sandy hair, the beauty mark on her right cheek, or her soft, velvety skin. It's a bitter realization, one that sits heavy on my heart as I write these words.

Your mother. We met in third-year Spanish class at college. I had taken four years in high school and another three in college, and I still struggled to master a second language. Your mother was nearly fluent. That's how she lives, striving for mastery and perfection in everything she does. We exchanged innocent glances during class and finally spoke for the first time when we recognized each other at a local bar. We were both in other relationships at the time, but looking back, it was evident there was an immediate connection. I was attracted to her New York accent, her piercing eyes, and her sense of humor. She is quick-witted and direct, unafraid to tell you how it is.

We remained friends and kept in touch after college. She attended grad school in Boston while I started a job teaching in Philadelphia. We'd talk on the phone well into the night, telling each other about our days and experiences as young adults trying to figure out the world without the security of college and family. I would travel to Boston to visit college friends and arrange to see her for coffee or lunch. I made several advances over those years, but each was refused. Your mother had other plans for us. She saw a future together and didn't want it tarnished amid the uncertainty of young adulthood. We were both still growing into the people we were striving to be.

After completing her dual degree in three years, your mother started looking for jobs all over the country. Call it chance or call it fate, she was offered a job in Philadelphia and relocated to the city I then called home. On a visit to look for an apartment, we spent some time together and shared our first kiss.

Letter 4

The highlight of our courtship is the tale of her meeting my family for the first time. I wanted her to accompany me to Uncle Ernie's wedding as my date. I convinced Uncle Ernie to meet her in Boston first. As he humorously recounted in his best man speech at our wedding, he went on the first date with your mother, where she drove, ordered salmon, and left a lasting impression. Upon meeting her, Ernie remarked, "David, she's great—funny and beautiful. Don't you think she's a bit too smart for you though?" He was right. Your mother is smarter than I could ever aspire to be. She "passed his test" and was my date at his wedding.

I definitely married up.

It would be nice to say, "The rest is history," but life doesn't unfold that way. Like any masterpiece, it requires hard work. Love may come easy, but creating and sharing a life together demands persistence, dedication, teamwork, compromise, compassion, patience, and understanding. The journey to build a life with your mother wasn't always smooth for me. There were struggles as I continued to mature and understand the depth of commitment and love.

Marriage, having children, and raising them together is a unique and special experience. Our journey together has been filled with challenges, yet the initial sparks of young passion grew into a blazing flame fueled by respect, friendship, and a love deeper than the physical realm. It ignited during long talks over the phone, sharing living spaces, planning a wedding, compromising on vacation destinations, and celebrating holidays with each other's families.

Our love flourished on runs through the Wissahickon Gorge, across the Ben Franklin Bridge, and along the Schuylkill River. It grew stronger as we started a family, rocking our babies through sleepless nights, wiping away tears, and witnessing all their firsts. This love was forged through joy, sorrow, and the unbearable pain of losing you, our precious child. There's no other person on this earth with whom

I would rather experience all of life's joy, sorrow, and pain than your mother.

Thank you, Charlie, for strengthening the love and bond between your mother and me. Wherever you are, understand this: your mother and I love you more than words can express.

Love,
Dad

Letter 4

Katherine and me, Ithaca College Graduation, May 2007

Katherine and me, NY Finger Lakes, July 2023

Letter 5

A mother's grief is as timeless as her love.

—Joanne Cacciatore

February 26, 2022

Dear Charlie,

Four months have passed since the day you were supposed to grace our lives with your laughter, a bundle of joy that never came to be. The world around us has changed in ways we could never have anticipated, and yet, the void left by your absence remains steadfast, an unwelcome companion in our daily lives.

Mom returned to work, a bittersweet decision that places her in the very halls where we first met you. She says it feels like you're with her every day. The memories, however, are a double-edged sword, cutting deep as she walks through the corridors of Labor and Delivery, surrounded by the sounds of life in the NICU. Mom finds solace in being at the hospital, a place that brings her closer to you, even amid the painful memories.

Letter 5

One day this month, a chance encounter unfolded. One of the three nurses who stood by her side during your delivery appeared in a patient room. Their shared sorrow wove an unspoken connection, a "Charlie Wink," as we've come to call these unexpected moments that remind us of you. They shared an embrace in the hallway afterward. The nurse said the entire unit was devastated the day you were born. Hearing this from the nurse gave Mom a sense of comfort, knowing you were on people's minds when you passed.

We also met with someone from Maternal Fetal Medicine, finalizing the investigation of your passing. It was both the closure of one chapter and the hesitant opening of another—talks about the possibility of trying for another baby. The emotions surrounding this prospect are tangled with guilt, whispering that considering another child is a betrayal. The sadness of trying for a baby without you here to share our love intensifies the struggle. Your brother William's birth taught us that love doesn't divide but multiplies and Alexander's arrival reinforced that truth. The love for all three of you grows immeasurably, and the thought of expanding our family is both daunting and hopeful, a delicate balance on the tightrope of grief.

During this meeting, we received the results of countless tests, each one shouting the same conclusion—nothing was amiss. Your mother's bloodwork and every examination were all normal. You, my precious one, were perfect in every way, save for the cruel twist of a true knot in your umbilical cord. The news, initially a spark of hope for a future sibling, became entangled with anger. The doctor's explanation, delivered with clinical precision, felt like salt in the wounds. The rage surged, a turbulent sea threatening to drown reason, as we learned that observing the umbilical cord in utero is an impossible task. No effective method exists, leaving us to navigate the dark waters of uncertainty. We also found little reassurance in the low likelihood of a repeat knot occurring in the next pregnancy.

Anger is a beast with gnashing teeth, a fire that rages within, scorching reason and leaving behind the charred remains of what once was. It's the frustration of being powerless, of knowing that the very life we long for hangs in the balance of statistical improbabilities. It's a primal scream in the face of an indifferent universe, a desperate plea for answers that remain elusive. It's a storm that brews in the darkest corners of the soul, threatening to consume everything in its path.

Hope and anger: two opposing forces pulling me in conflicting directions. Your mother and I, still caught in the undertow of shock and disbelief, have yet to decide to try for another baby. The choice looms, heavy and laden with emotion, as we grapple with the dichotomy of yearning for a new life while mourning the one we lost.

And then, a box arrived, a vessel of unexpected hope. Within rested a silver bear, a scarlet bow tie around its neck, and a train embroidered across its belly. It weighed precisely 6 lbs. 15 ounces, mirroring your birth weight. The note from the compassionate soul who crafted it conveyed a depth of understanding born from their own sorrow. Molly Bears, a company forged in the crucible of loss, gifted us this tangible connection to you. Your brothers, radiant in their love and compassion, unwrapped the bear with the fervor of Christmas morning. The tears flowed freely as we held the bear, its weight a poignant reminder of what should have been. Happiness and joy mingled with sorrow and pain, a complex symphony echoing the multifaceted nature of our grief.

Thank you, Charlie, for guiding these unexpected gifts into our lives. Your spirit, woven into the fabric of our family, continues to teach us profound lessons about love, resilience, and the intricate dance of emotions that accompany loss. The

Letter 5

waves of happiness, sorrow, anger, and frustration crash over us daily, a testament to the enduring impact of your brief presence in our lives.

As we navigate this uncharted terrain, please continue to send your "winks" from wherever you are. Your love, a beacon in the darkness, remains our guiding light.

Love,
Dad

Dear Charlie...Letters To My Son

Charlie Bear on beach with us

Letter 6

No one ever told me that grief felt so like fear.

—C.S. Lewis

March 11, 2022

Dear Charlie,

A few months before you were born, William approached me with a heavy question. It was a warm August evening. We were playing outside. Your mom was seven months pregnant with you. I was about to travel to Boston the next morning for work, the first time I'd spend a night away from William. As we cleaned up to head in for the night, William, placing his gardening tools away, looked up at me with concern.

"Dad, are we going to lose you?"

Confused, I responded, "Lose me? What do you mean, bud?"

"Like, lose you."

Perplexed, I pressed, "I'm right here. How can you lose me?"

"Are we going to lose you like we lost big grandpap?"

His words clarified the fear that lingered in his young mind. He was worried about me traveling, a concern rooted in the recent loss of my grandfather, big grandpap, who had passed away the previous February. At that moment, I paused, feeling a knot in my stomach as I realized he was asking if I might die.

"It seems like you're thinking about something. Are you worrying about me traveling tomorrow?"

"Yeah," he nodded.

"It's okay to worry when people travel by plane. Flying can be scary. You understand. You've been in an airplane before. I don't think you're going to lose me tomorrow, though."

"But we'll lose you someday, right?"

I took a deep breath, bracing myself for the weight of the conversation. Kneeling in front of William, I said, "Yes, bud. Someday, you will lose me. I hope it's not for a very, very long time, though."

Tears welled up in his eyes, and he began to cry. I hugged him tightly as tears fell from my own eyes.

Over the following weeks, William asked more questions about death. Explaining mortality to a five-year-old isn't easy, but it's a part of growing up. Parents find themselves weaving stories to cushion the harsh truth. Who wants to talk about dying with their five-year-old? Your mom is a child psychologist, and I'm an educator. We've learned through our careers and training that the best thing for children (and the easiest thing for adults) is to tell the truth—be simple, be concrete, and be honest. Here's a glimpse of those conversations:

William: "Why do we die?"

Me: "As we grow older, our bodies start to get tired. They break down, and eventually, parts of them stop working. When our heart stops, we die."

William: "What happens when you die?"

Me: "No one knows for sure, bud. Our religion teaches us you go to heaven when you die. Other people believe

Letter 6

different things, like coming back to life or returning as an animal. Some believe nothing happens."

William: "When will I die? When will you die?"

Me: "You're thinking a lot about this. No one knows exactly when they will die. I hope both of us are very, very old when we die, like big grandpap. He was 92 years old."

Children, especially at William's age, revisit these questions, seeking consistency in their understanding. August passed with William raising these concerns periodically, and I offered consistent answers, creating a narrative for his young mind.

Little did we know a few months later, we would have to tell William you had passed away. It was a challenging day, deciding how to inform the boys. When we left for the hospital, we told them you might be on the way. At that point, they believed they would meet their new sibling soon. But reality hit, and we realized we had to share the painful truth.

Some at the hospital advised us not to say anything to the boys, but that seemed impossible. They knew you were expected, and silence would only fuel confusion. Child Life Specialists, professionals your mom works with at the hospital, guided us. Child Life Specialists are health professionals who assist children and their families during emotional experiences such as surgery, hospitalization, tests, and procedures. They've discovered that when children understand what is happening to them, they cope more effectively and experience less psychological anxiety and trauma. Child Life Specialists are trained in child development, child life, education, and psychology. In our conversations with them, they emphasized simplicity, honesty, and waiting for questions, understanding that kids process information at different rates and in different ways than adults.

Returning home that evening was surreal, the house quiet despite family around. William and Alexander played in the living room, eagerly awaiting news of their new brother. After saying goodbye to you at the hospital, seeing them brought relief. They shared their creations with enthusiasm but then came the pause.

"Where's the baby? Is he here?" William asked excitedly.

Inhaling deeply, your mom explained, "Oh, William. The baby isn't here. He's not coming home." Another breath. "He died."

Silence fell. William stopped playing, Alexander looked up with curiosity, and questions followed.

"What ... what happened?" William asked.

Glancing at your mom, her eyes welling with tears, I replied, "His heart stopped while he was in mommy's belly."

"Where's baby now?" Alexander questioned.

"He is safe at a funeral home. They are keeping him nice and comfortable for us. We're going to see him tomorrow. Would you like to see him?"

William nodded.

"I want to see baby," Alexander said.

"We can all go see him together," Mom assured.

More silence enveloped us. Alexander resumed building with tiles, and William climbed into your mom's lap. I started building tiles with Alexander.

"What's his name?" William asked after a while.

"Good question," your mom said. "His name is Charlie. Charles Martin Corvi."

William began crying, softly at first, then louder. Alexander, noticing William's sadness, approached, offering comfort and understanding.

"It's okay, Winning." (Alexander pronounces William as "Winning") "We'll go see baby Charlie tomorrow." We sat there for several minutes, embracing and comforting each other. The evening passed in a similar fashion. Your grandparents and my siblings had arrived to help in any way they could.

Letter 6

The following morning, as we gathered for breakfast, William's inquisitive nature persisted. He sought consistency in our explanations, attempting to grasp the reality of your passing.

"Baby Charlie died, right?" he asked.

"Yea, bud. He did," I replied.

"What happened?"

"Well, his . . ." I began.

"And don't say his heart stopped beating," William interrupted. "How did he die? What happened to him?"

Your mom looked to me for answers. After a moment of contemplation, I reached for a blank piece of paper and a pencil. With a few strokes, I created a circle and a stick figure inside.

"This circle is mommy's belly. And inside the circle is Charlie. This was him inside mommy's belly." I drew a line starting from your belly and connecting it to the outside of the circle. "When you're in mommy's belly, you don't breathe like you do right now. You don't eat or drink the same, either. You eat, drink, and breathe through what is called an umbilical cord, a tube connected to mommy through your belly button. Everyone has a belly button. Where's your belly button?" William lifted his shirt and pointed. "Right. Where's my belly button?" He playfully poked me in the belly, and we shared a brief giggle.

Continuing, I explained, "When Charlie was moving around in mommy's belly, he got himself tangled up a bit around his umbilical cord. It got tied into a knot and then wrapped around his ankle." I illustrated the line wrapping around your ankle and into a twist. "On Monday morning, the knot closed off, which closed the tube going from him to mommy." I marked an X over the twist in the line. "He couldn't eat, drink, or breathe then. When you can't breathe, your heart stops. And when your heart stops . . ."

" . . . you die," William softly concluded.

"Right, bud. And that is how Charlie died."

William started crying and embraced me. I let my own tears fall as I held him close to me.

Kids grieve, too. Even without the words to express their emotions fully, they feel the void, and they experience a unique journey of loss. Our therapist assures us that William and Alexander will continue to navigate their understanding of losing you as they grow older. It's a process that unfolds, never truly reaching an end.

Wherever you are and whatever you're doing, please know you are loved and missed more than anything.

Love,
Dad

Letter 6

Drawing for William and Alexander explaining how Charlie died

Letter 7

> Wherever you find yourself today, I hope that God will meet you in your place of pain. That he will sit in your brokenness with you as only another bereaved parent can.
>
> —Rachel Lewis

March 24, 2022

Dear Charlie,

 I'm retracing the steps of my past today, and my thoughts are drawn to Tihomir Teisl, fondly known as Tiho, my high school soccer coach and Spanish teacher. Tiho, a fixture in the school community for over four decades, left a mark on my life during those formative years. He recently died from cancer, bringing a profound sense of loss to my high school and echoing the intricate threads of connection that tie our lives together.

 Tiho was more than an educator; he was a guide, a mentor, and a presence that transcended the boundaries of the classroom. Even post-graduation, our paths remained connected. He attended our wedding and always offered wisdom

Letter 7

whenever I sought advice on my journey as an educator, high school teacher, and athletic coach.

But what truly amazed me was the depth of Tiho's resilience in the face of adversity. Despite the unimaginable loss of his youngest son, Christopher, at the age of two, Tiho persevered and found strength in guiding his other children through the journey of life. He continued to raise three living boys, each a testament to his unwavering commitment to fatherhood. When you were born, I couldn't help but think of Tiho and his family, wondering about the intricate web of grief and resilience that defined his existence.

The questions that occupy my thoughts reflect those that surely troubled Tiho—how do I navigate life after losing a child? How do I uphold faith and spirituality in the face of profound loss? As the morning sun rises, carrying the weight of grief, I wrestle with an indifference to my spirituality and faith. It's not anger or fervent recommitment; it's a profound sense of numbness, an emotional callus shielding me from the raw pain of your absence.

Sundays find us in the quiet embrace of mass, a tradition woven within the rhythm of life and death, a familiar cadence from my Catholic upbringing. In this space, I seek refuge amid the rituals, attempting to bridge the gap between this world and the next, yearning for closeness to you. My belief in God and an afterlife persists, but the inexplicable tragedy of losing you makes it challenging to reconcile and comprehend the grand design of existence.

The age-old questions echo through time, resonating within my soul—why did this happen? Why to you, to your mother, to your brothers, to our family? The fragility of our human condition presents us with the stark reality of mortality, a reality I've grappled with since childhood. At 37, I still wake in the dead of night, gripped by the fear that one day, the breath of life will cease within me.

Tiho's faith and dedication extended beyond his family. He founded, coordinated, organized, and led annual service trips to Nuevo Paradiso, a community outside the capital city of Tegucigalpa, Honduras. This endeavor showcased not only his leadership skills but also his compassionate heart, reaching out to those in need and inspiring others to join him in making a positive impact.

His influence didn't end there. Tiho remained a prominent figure in Ohio's high school soccer scene, coaching for over thirty seasons and becoming a well-known and respected coach. His commitment to the sport mirrored his resilience in the face of personal tragedy, showcasing a remarkable ability to channel grief into motivation and strength.

In the midst of life's challenges, Tiho maintained his devotion to family. He remained committed to his wife, weathering the storms of life by her side. Even after her passing, he carried their shared memories and love, outliving her by several years.

Tiho's presence continued to resonate within the school community. He remained engaged with the world, serving as a source of motivation and inspiration to students and colleagues alike. His enduring spirit after the loss of Christopher became a beacon of hope, illustrating that even in the face of profound sorrow, we can find purpose and resilience.

As I grapple with my own grief, Tiho's life becomes a testament to the strength within the human spirit. His ability to navigate loss, raise a family, contribute to the well-being of others, and remain engaged with the world serves as a source of awe and inspiration. I find comfort in the knowledge that amid the shadows of tragedy, individuals like Tiho are guiding lights who illuminate the path forward. Thoughts of him and his resilience act as a compass through the dense fog of loss. The shared experiences of losing a child, an unthinkable tragedy, form an intricate web that ties us together. We've

Letter 7

discovered, perhaps unexpectedly, that the vastness of this pain is not solitary; it's a burden carried by many.

Loss is a universal thread that binds us all, transcending race, religion, and nationality. Through our connection to remarkable individuals who endure with purpose, we catch a glimpse of the silver lining you've gifted us. Your untimely departure has led us to a community of resilient souls who comprehend the depth of our sorrow in its rawest form.

Thank you, my dear Charlie, for guiding us to these extraordinary souls.

Wherever you are in the vast expanse of eternity, know your mother and I are filled with an unwavering affection for you that eclipses the boundaries of time and space.

Love,
Dad

Tiho Teisl, Honduras, April 2003

Letter 8

Grief can be a burden, but also an anchor.
You get used to the weight, how it holds you in place.

—Sarah Dessen

April 13, 2022

Dear Charlie,

    In the aftermath of your passing, the notion of escaping our daily reality, even momentarily, became a crucial form of therapy and coping. The weight of grief was both a relentless storm and a persistent fog. We sought respite—a temporary sanctuary where joy could momentarily outweigh sorrow. Two weeks ago, during William's spring break, we embarked on a journey that many people encouraged.
    Where did we go? The place synonymous with childhood magic and joy—Disney World, of course. Yet, as we immersed ourselves in the enchanting world of imagination, the waves of happiness and joy were immediately followed by the crashing tides of anger and sadness. It struck me, Charlie, that you will never experience the innocent delights that come from watching a Disney movie: memorizing lines,

singing all the songs, and dancing around the house with William, Alexander, Mom, and me. The unfairness of it all is maddening.

    I'm writing this letter, like the many others, not only to express my gratitude but also to acknowledge your presence in our family narrative. Thank you for being the reason we ventured to Florida. Despite the underlying sorrow, you became the catalyst for a shared experience—a therapeutic journey for the four of us. Rest assured, you were with us, just as you are every day. We brought along Charlie Bear, tucked safely in one of our backpacks. The encounter with a TSA agent at the security checkpoint added a touch of humor and anxiety as the stuffed bear underwent a thorough pat-down. Thankfully, he emerged on the other side of the X-ray machine in one piece. The clear blue skies and 80-degree Florida weather were a welcome change from the drudgery of the gray and cold winters in Northeast Ohio. As we navigated the charming parks, it became a pilgrimage of sorts, an intentional act of healing in the face of profound loss.

    Absence could have cast a shadow over every smile and laughter, a stark reminder of the void that can never be filled. Yet, we find that when we acknowledge the loss, we grapple with this new reality that cannot be changed. We make an effort to plan for a future where you are not physically present but always with us. We understand the impact of your loss on our lives, relationships, and trajectory. Each morning in Disney World, we'd secure Charlie Bear in my backpack and set off to explore the magical parks. Armed with a Memory Maker photo pass, we captured moments at various locations where cast members took our photograph. The ritual of pulling out Charlie Bear for a family photo became a noteworthy part of our adventure.

    In this attempt at acknowledging your death, we strive to find meaning anew, to feel more secure and relaxed despite the weight of sorrow. We engage with reality as it is, not as we

Letter 8

once thought it would be. Every moment in Disney World became a testament to the bittersweet acknowledgment that life must still go on, even in your absence.

As we posed for family photos with Charlie Bear, an unspoken communication emerged, an acknowledgment of your perpetual existence within our hearts. Interestingly, no one inquired about the bear. Your mother and I have struggled with how to respond when asked about the number of children we have. Despite rehearsing simple responses, the moment always catches us off guard. Do we share? How much? What will their reaction be? What will *our* reaction be? The conflict arises from the desire to celebrate your existence while grappling with the emotional toll it takes in the moment.

On the last day of our trip, the moment we both dreaded and longed for came: the first photographer asked about Charlie Bear. I once again witnessed the remarkable courage of your mother. Without hesitation, she proudly declared, "It's our third son!" The photographer, moved by her response, offered his sympathies. In that moment, we all found strength and a newfound ability to communicate openly and assertively about our grief. That day at Animal Kingdom became the highlight of our vacation—an embodiment of acknowledgment, communication, and comfort amid the complexities of grief.

Thank you, Charlie. Thank you.

Wherever you are and whatever you are doing, please know your mother and I love you more than anything.

Love,
Dad

Dear Charlie...Letters To My Son

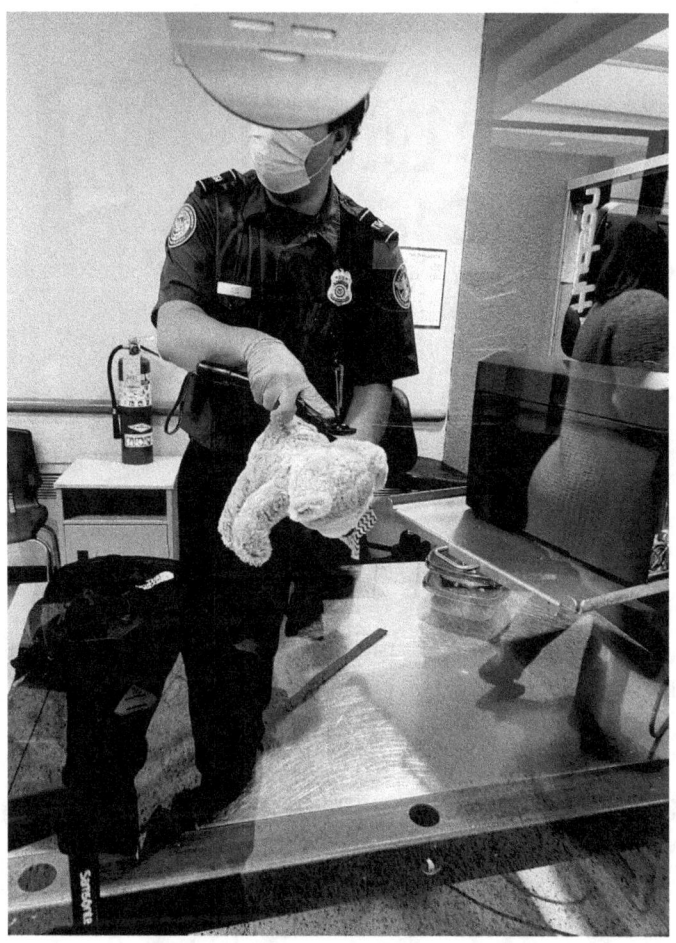

Charlie Bear going through security at airport

Letter 9

> Come to me, all you who are weary and burdened,
> and I will give you rest.
>
> —Matthew 11:28

May 12, 2022

Dear Charlie,

    Mom is pregnant. So much is running through my mind right now. How do I tell you? Should I tell you? What do I tell you? What does it mean for you? What does it mean for us? It's insane to think that just eight months ago, we were eagerly anticipating your arrival. Now your mother's pregnant again, and you're gone.
    Like always, it's multiple emotions at the same time. Joy for the baby. Sorrow for your loss. Anger that this happened to you. All of it is wrapped up in a big bow of anxiety and stress about how this pregnancy will go.
    Mom had her eight-week appointment a few days ago. I parked in the same lot I parked in the night you were born. I crossed the same walkway to the hospital. Sat in the same waiting room where we last heard your heartbeat. Mom's

doctor came into the exam room. We could immediately tell he, too, was experiencing multiple emotions. He embraced us and said congratulations.

We've become very close with him. Mom works with his wife, who is also a doctor. He was there the night you died when he came running into the triage room, out of breath from sprinting across the hospital. He confirmed your heart had stopped. He stayed with us the whole night and took a nap in the room next door so he could be on call to deliver you. He cried with us when you were born. He and his wife attended your funeral. We soon learned afterward that his daughter also lost a child in a similar manner. He referred us to the therapist his family saw; she has been wonderful for your mom and me. Now, here he was, celebrating with us and comforting us as we waited to listen for your sibling's heartbeat. You've left such an impact on so many people.

The ultrasound machine. It stood there waiting, towering over me as I sat in a low chair next to Mom in the exam bed. I couldn't stop looking at it as I anxiously waited for the exam to begin. That's the machine where we first saw your still heart. Despite the graininess of the monitor, the image is so clearly imprinted in my mind: your heart not beating. All the emotions of that day came flooding back into that exam room. I looked at your mother, who I could tell was thinking and feeling the exact same. The doctor started the exam, turning the monitor so we couldn't see it. He was holding his breath. He took the first look, a simple act I greatly appreciated. His compassion and professionalism were on full display in that simple gesture of protecting us, being the first to look so he could prepare us for what we were about to see.

Was your sibling's heart beating?

He exhaled, smiled, and turned the screen toward us. "There it is!" The grainy image came into our view. There

Letter 9

was the baby's heart. Fluttering quickly. Your mother reached for my hand. We were both crying. Tears for all sorts of emotions—happiness for the health of your sibling, grief for our loss of you, relief for your sibling's safety.

It was an exhausting visit. William and Alexander don't know yet. We're worried about William's reaction when we do tell him Mom is pregnant. He's such an incredibly observant, thoughtful, cerebral kid. He will immediately ask and worry about whether this baby will die, too. He loves and misses you so much. Last week, he had a few days of pretty severe behavior—short temper, irritability, not really listening, not being kind to Alexander. It took Mom and me a few days to figure it out. Mom asked him, "William, what have you been feeling?" He responded, "I'm sad because of Charlie. I miss him." In that moment, an incredible weight lifted from his shoulders. Mom hugged him. His mood and behavior immediately improved. He just needed to share he was missing you.

Alexander, too. He's still home with me on Mondays and Fridays, going to daycare Tuesdays through Thursdays. I've been trying really hard to be in the moment and cherish these days with him. He'll start daycare five days a week this summer, so I only have a handful left when it's just him and me. Last week, he was eating a Dum Dum lollipop, and he told me he wanted to share some with you. He walked over to your urn and offered you a lick. "Here you go, Baby Charlie. Do you like it? It's my favorite."

Joy and hope. Sorrow and anger. We navigate this intricate dance of emotions, seeking positivity and comfort amid the tears and frustration. In this maelstrom of intensity, there's a thread of optimism weaving through the tapestry of our experience. I will never feel happy about the loss. Rather, I find an understanding in the pain and loss experienced, and I start to look forward to and plan for the future. This next step in our journey is about coming to terms with the fact that our new reality cannot be changed, and we have to figure out how this new reality will impact our lives, relationships, and trajectories.

Wherever you are and whatever you're doing, know you are loved and missed more than anything.

Love,
Dad

Letter 9

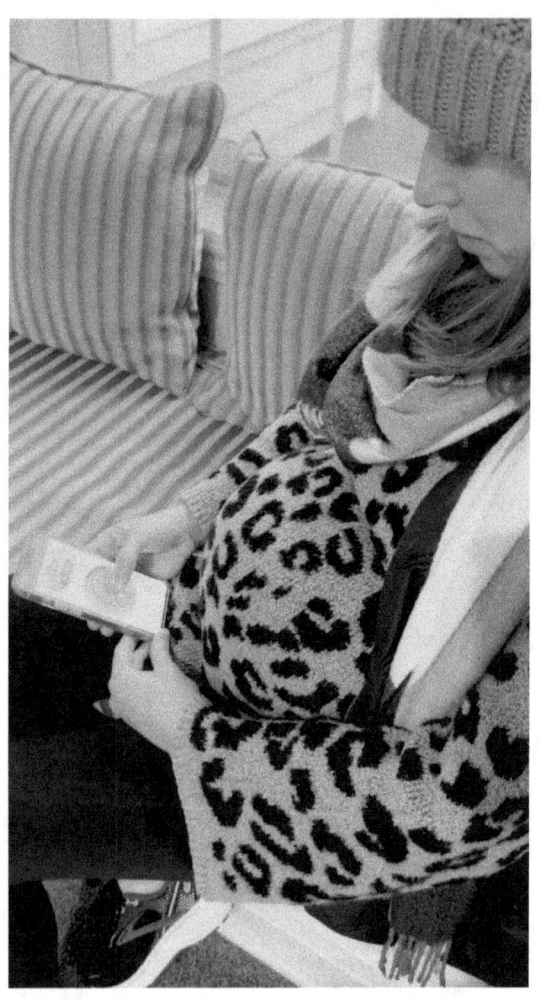

Katherine pregnant with Louis using the Count The Kicks app

Letter 10

I hope this grief stays with me because it's all the unexpressed love I didn't get to tell her.

—Andrew Garfield

May 17, 2022

Dear Charlie,

 In a serene cemetery in Salt Lake City, Utah, stands an angel statue, a symbol of solace. This statue was commissioned by Richard Paul Evans, who wrote *The Christmas Box*. The novel tells of the grief a widowed mother experiences while coping with the loss of her three-year-old daughter. Within the narrative, this angelic sculpture serves as a modest yet emotional headstone for the departed daughter. On each anniversary of her daughter's death, the grieving mother tenderly visits the statue, places a single flower in the angel's arms, and explores her grief in the quiet moments of reflection.

 Following the book's release, one question lingered in readers' minds: did the statue truly exist? Responding to the inquiries, the author took a heartfelt step—the angel statue

Letter 10

was commissioned and brought into tangible existence. It is characterized by its perch on a stone pedestal, the angel's wings extending gracefully behind her, and her arms outstretched as though poised for a tender embrace with an invisible presence. Since its dedication in December of 1994, this sacred monument has drawn grieving parents from all corners of the world who seek peace and connection in the quietness of the Utah landscape. After your untimely departure, we dove into the pages of *The Christmas Box*. The angelic statue, a central motif in the book, became a poignant symbol for your mother and me during the weeks following your birth and departure from our lives.

As we explored the narrative, we uncovered a heartening revelation—more than 120 replica angel statues inspired by the book have been created and generously donated to children's cemeteries across the nation. Remarkably, these angelic sentinels also found homes in Canada and Japan. Close to us, a mere five miles south of our Ohio residence, a replica angel statue stands in the back right corner of a children's cemetery in Stow, Ohio. Facing southeast, this angel presides over the resting places of children who departed their parents and families far too soon. Commissioned and dedicated in 2002, the Stow Christmas Box Angel graces a circular path covered with red brick pavers, each etched with the names and dates of hundreds of children who have passed away, a touching tribute to their enduring memory.

Through the generosity of William's school, a humble yet heartfelt tribute took the form of a brick dedicated in your memory. The inscription reads:

In Memory of
Charles Martin Corvi
October 26, 2021

This brick finds itself in a prominent position, situated front and center of the angel statue. It offers a beautiful view of the angel with her arms gracefully outstretched.

In a tender ceremony hosted last December by the Friends of the Christmas Box Angel committee, we joined others in illuminating candles in front of the statue to honor the lives of our lost children. This event is known as the Wave of Light and is recognized across the globe. More recently, on Sunday, May 15th, your brick found its place alongside those of 20 other newly cherished children, forming a mosaic of remembrance. With a deep sense of purpose, I have actively engaged with the committee, contributing my time and effort. From assisting in the planning of the ceremony to reading a heartfelt poem titled "Because You're Not Here," I find support and meaning in these moments of commemoration.

Navigating the grief journey and parenting a child we've lost becomes an intricate dance, an ongoing dialogue between your mother and me. The inability to capture moments like your first steps or first words, to witness the sparkle in your eyes as you taste your first birthday cake, or to share the enchantment of your first snowfall are all profound losses. We are robbed of the joy found in opening your first Christmas presents or witnessing the nervous excitement of your first day of school. Youth activities, drop-offs at friends' houses, the tender act of dusting you off and embracing you after a fall—these are experiences we long for but will never have. We can't scold you, guide you to have kind hands and words with your brothers, or lie beside you while rubbing your back and humming you to sleep. The question lingers, how do we continue to parent you, expressing our love and care, when you are not physically here?

In a gesture of love and remembrance, we extended invitations to family and friends for the brick ceremony at the Christmas Box Angel statue. Catering food and gathering

Letter 10

everyone back at our home, we collectively celebrated the impact you've had on so many lives.

Our connection with you persists in various ways. We engage in conversations with you, whispering good morning and good night as if the air carries our words to you. Your presence is acknowledged with a constant place setting at the dinner table and your picture nestled beside the boys' school photos. As a tangible tribute, I'm crafting a cedar chest to safeguard your cherished belongings. Your name graces thank-you notes and cards, a signature of love and remembrance. Our marathon team bears your name, a testament to the enduring impact you've had. We continue to feel your presence during therapy, where we process the depth of our loss. Tears flow freely as your mother and I hold each other during these "Charlie Moments."

Your story, your essence, is shared with everyone we know, an ongoing narrative that echoes our love for you. In these myriad ways, we continue to parent you, finding peace and expression for the love that endures.

The narrator in *The Christmas Box* grapples with a familiar dilemma that strikes all parents—imbalances between work and family, self-care, and being present for their children. He is a father, ensnared in the pursuit of professional success, finding himself neglecting valuable moments with his young daughter. Through tender interactions with the widowed and grieving mother, he gradually unravels the profound gift within his daughter and the irreplaceable time he is missing. This narrative reflects a universal struggle faced by parents across diverse cultures and throughout the tapestry of human history. The challenge of a balanced life has inspired numerous books and movies, emphasizing the enduring relevance of this theme.

In contemplating this struggle, Pope Francis, during confessions with parents, consistently poses a question: "How much time do you spend playing with your children?" This query transcends religious boundaries, resonating as a timeless reminder of the importance of quality time spent with our loved ones.

While being part of The Christmas Box Angel committee introduces an added layer of sorrow into my heart, I cannot deny the gratitude that coexists. Dedicated to this work, I find an unexpected avenue to be your parent once again, an opportunity to express and demonstrate my enduring love for you. Charlie, in your absence, I am thankful for this chance to continue being your dad.

Wherever you find yourself and whatever occupies your moments, know your mother and I harbor a love for you that surpasses anything imaginable.

Love,
Dad

Letter 10

Christmas Box Angel of Hope Statue with Charlie's brick, Stow, Ohio

Dear Charlie...Letters To My Son

Christmas Box Angel of Hope Statue, Stow, Ohio

Charlie's brick with penny, Stow, Ohio

Letter 11

The only true wisdom is in knowing you know nothing.

—Socrates

June 23, 2022

Dear Charlie,

One year before your anticipated arrival, our lives underwent a seismic shift. We left our home outside Philadelphia, Pennsylvania, amid the unfolding pandemic. Your mother and I, with plans to try for a third child, found ourselves reevaluating as society grappled with the escalating threat of COVID-19.

The worldwide crisis impacted my job, prompting us to sell our Pennsylvania home and seek new opportunities. Remarkably, your incredible mother received several job offers, ultimately choosing to work at a hospital in Ohio. That July, we listed our house and embarked on multiple trips in search of our new home. We decided to postpone expanding our family until we were settled. Our official move took place in October 2020, marking the beginning of a busy period—finding schools for the boys, starting new jobs, making our house a home, and acquainting ourselves with our new community. Still, we waited.

What if COVID had never happened? You might have been with us a year earlier, and this tragedy may never have befallen you.

What if we had stayed in Pennsylvania? You would have been born at the same hospital as William and Alexander, and this sorrow might have been averted.

What if we had chosen a different place to live? Ohio's high infant mortality rate looms large. Had I accepted the job in Massachusetts, perhaps this heartbreak would have been spared.

What if Mom's health wasn't as robust? Standards of excellent health during pregnancy didn't raise any concerns. What if abnormalities had been detected?

What if medical practices were different? Physicians don't routinely monitor for knots and loops in the umbilical cord. Could earlier detection have changed the outcome?

What if Mom had made different dietary choices or altered her activity level during pregnancy? There is a heavy guilt she carries with her.

What if...

What if...

What if...

During these "what if" scenarios, desperation creeps in, a yearning to change the past, to strike a deal that could somehow alter our present reality. Negotiating with fate becomes a subconscious plea for a different outcome.

In the aftermath of losing a child, the mind becomes entangled in a web of possible realities that could have been ours. Your mom carries the constant, 24/7 reminder of you within her body. She experienced a phase of grief where she questioned her body and lost trust in its capacity to create and nurture life. Your selfless, compassionate, and considerate

Letter 11

mother bears the brunt of losing you while I, perhaps less burdened, still grapple with my own complexities.

The human mind is intricate and can be incredibly fragile at times, capable of conjuring thoughts that traverse wild and haunting scenarios. The most painful image my mind paints is of you lying lifeless on the scale in our hospital room. Six pounds and 15 ounces—a delicate figure. Your right arm rests on your belly, a silent testimony to the life that could have been. The nurse gently takes your left handprint. Your pale skin, still glistening from delivery, remains forever closed off to sensing the wonders of this world. I would do anything to give you another chance at life.

Wherever you are and whatever you may be doing, please know you are loved and missed more than words can express.

Love,
David

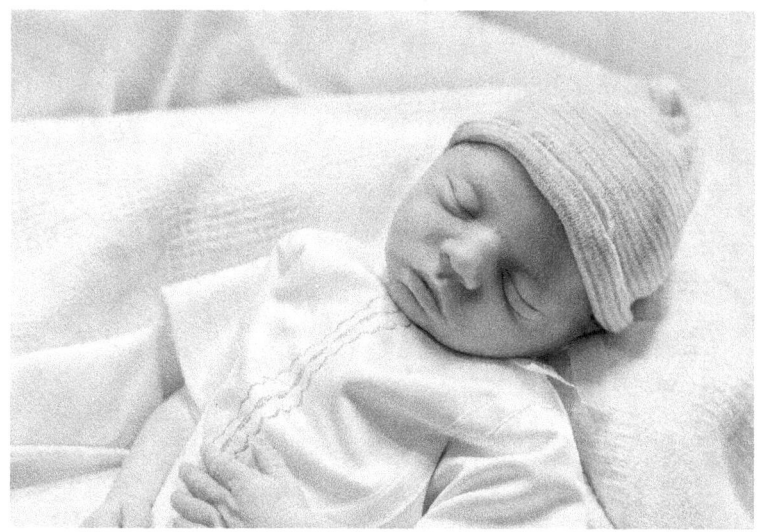

Charlie, Now I Lay Me Down To Sleep, Marti Wagner

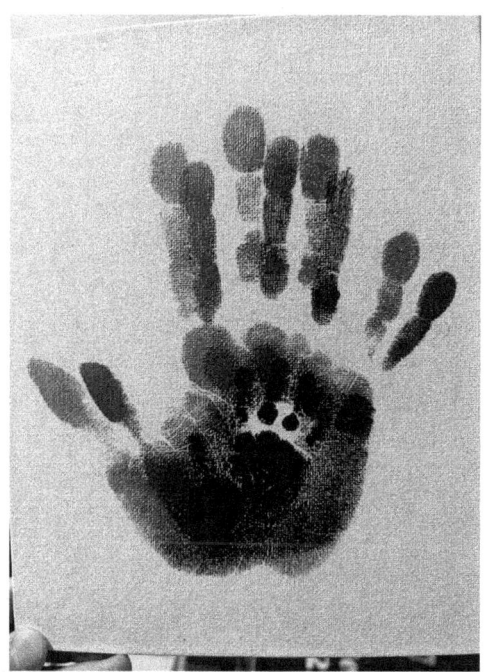

Charlie's hand prints layered with Katherine's and mine

Letter 12

*Children are not only innocent and curious
but also optimistic and joyful and essentially happy.
They are, in short, everything adults wish they could be.*

—Carolyn Haywood

July 7, 2022

Dear Charlie,

William celebrated his sixth birthday last week. For his special day, he insisted on Chick-fil-A for dinner and chose the decorations for his birthday cake—a hockey rink complete with a puck, goal, and goaltender. We gathered around after dinner, decorated the cake with six multi-colored candles, and belted out our off-key version of "Happy Birthday." As he closed his eyes for a moment before blowing out the candles, we couldn't help but wonder about the wish he harbored.

Although there's a superstition that suggests wishes should be kept secret for them to come true, we were interested when William asked, "Do you want to know what I wished for?" With anticipation, we nodded.

"I wished that Charlie was alive."

A week later, during our vacation exploring Forsyth Park in Savannah, Georgia, William stumbled upon a penny on the ground. Some say finding a coin is a sign from those who have passed away. In the heart of the park, surrounded by ancient oak trees with hanging southern moss, stands a 150-year-old fountain. William, holding the penny in his little hand, decided to toss it into the fountain. The penny sailed over the wrought iron fence, creating a small splash. As he closed his eyes and covered them with both hands, he whispered, "I wish Charlie was alive."

Feelings of anger permeate this letter, a deep-seated emotion that simmers beneath the surface. Anger not directed at you, dear Charlie, but at the cruel reality that you will never have the chance to meet your brothers.

William and Alexander express their love for you in so many ways:

Alexander, with his caring nature, often says he wants to give you a hug. He embraces the Charlie Chimes, those sweet sounds echoing the love he has for the brother he never got to meet.

William, active and compassionate, aided in planting the blue spruce evergreen in our Charlie Garden. Each dig of the shovel, a symbol of his dedication to ensuring your memory thrives.

In a tender moment, Alexander shares a lick of his lollipop with a breeze as if offering a taste to you, his unseen but not unfelt companion.

William, the cautious older brother, isn't afraid to show his vulnerability. He cries openly because he misses you, the pain evident in each teardrop that falls.

Alexander, the adventurous and caring younger brother, takes it upon himself to introduce you to every new person he encounters. Your name becomes a part of his daily

Letter 12

conversations, a testament to the permanent mark you've left on his heart.

William, in a simple yet moving gesture, leaves toys by your urn on our mantel. It's his way of ensuring you're not forgotten in the midst of our daily lives.

Alexander, with his affectionate nature, lovingly refers to you as "Baby Charlie," a term that echoes with warmth and love whenever he says it.

William, grappling with his emotions, seeks solace in therapy and a grief camp. It's a brave step, a reflection of his commitment to understanding and navigating the complex emotions tied to your absence.

Alexander, the youngest but not the least caring, expresses his love by wanting to sleep with Charlie Bear, which he lovingly calls "Baby Charlie." The bear becomes a cherished companion, a tangible connection to the brother he'll never physically meet.

Both boys assist in pulling the weeds that have grown in your garden. It's a collaborative effort, symbolic of the shared responsibility they feel towards maintaining the space dedicated to you.

In the midst of our grieving, anger is constantly present in the harsh reality that you won't have the opportunity to witness the growing love and bond between your brothers. It's a complex emotion simmering beneath the surface, echoing a sense of injustice that you won't be there to share in the laughter, tears, and milestones with William and Alexander.

No matter where you are or what you're doing, know you are profoundly missed and loved.

Love,
Dad

Charlie's Garden

Charlie's Garden

Letter 12

Fountain at Forsyth Park, Savannah, Georgia

Letter 13

> Waste no more time arguing about
> what a good man should be. Be one.
>
> —Marcus Aurelius

August 6, 2022

Dear Charlie,

    I hope this letter reaches you surrounded by the timeless embrace of love. As I sit down to write, memories of my maternal grandfather come flooding back. He was a significant presence in my early years, a figure of strength and resilience, much like the love I carry for you. He was a tower of a person, having to duck his head and turn his shoulders to fit through the doorways of his home. My dad once described his father-in-law as the toughest and strongest person he ever knew. And this wasn't in the figurative sense. My dad meant this quite literally.

    My grandfather embodied the mid-20th century American man, a self-made entrepreneur in construction and excavation. His hands crafted not only structures but also memories. He built his house with his own hands—a cape

Letter 13

cod-style structure nestled into the side of a hill off Route 40, also known as National Road, in Bridgeport, Ohio. A house he raised six children in, my mother the youngest. The scent of sizzling bacon and homemade wine, the sight of chicken rotisseries in the backyard—all of these linger in my mind.

A man of the earth, he hunted, grew his own tomatoes and grapes, and shared his love of fishing with me. I recall the joy of one trip, the excitement in his eyes, and his deep laugh as I reeled in a large-mouth bass. He thought my hook was caught on a log. We shared the catch for dinner, a simple yet profound connection to the cycles of life and nature. During our visits, the second-floor landing of his house became a playground, connected by a crawl space that sparked our imagination. The cement stairwell on the outside of his house doubled as a mountain to climb in our youthful adventures. Toys from fast-food meals covered the kitchen table, providing endless entertainment for his grandchildren.

Life took him from construction to the steel mills of the Ohio River Valley. Clad in a silver fireproof suit, he balanced atop blast furnaces, transforming iron ore into molten metal. A stroke later in life left him with limited mobility, yet he ingeniously rigged a system to drive using only the left side of his body. The image of him living alone following the tragic loss of my grandmother remains etched in my memory.

I can still hear my mom's voice as she referred to him as Daddy. She remembers her father as a man's man: a husband with the responsibility to provide for his family's physical safety and well-being. He would play Italian or Polka music in the kitchen after Sunday church. Despite his tough exterior, the aging process and health challenges softened his resilience. The decision to place him in a nursing home, necessitated by his declining mobility, marked a significant chapter in our family's journey.

As I recount these memories, one particular moment stands out—the wedding of my cousin, an event my grandfather couldn't physically attend. Yet, the love of family bridged the gap. The bridal couple, complete in a tuxedo and dress, came to the nursing home to bring the celebration to him. Witnessing this, I saw a crack in my grandfather's armor, a vulnerability that transcended a lifetime of strength and stoicism. I was in high school at the time.

The depth of this vulnerability became starkly evident when the festivities ended, and the bridal party moved on for photos. My cousin's departure triggered a torrent of emotions in my grandfather. Shattering the facade of a lifetime of invincibility, he wept uncontrollably. I can only imagine the overwhelming wave of loneliness, fear, and sadness that engulfed him as my mom and aunts tried to comfort him. A life of being the toughest and strongest of men, of being the rock to his family, of burying his wife, of holding it all together, came crashing down because he had to be alone while one of his grandchildren got married.

He passed away several years later while I was In college. I didn't return home for his funeral. I don't have a good excuse. I was wrapped up in the egocentric mind and tunnel vision of a 20-year-old. It's a regret I carry with me and think about often.

And now, in the current sea of grief, I grapple with the chinks in my own armor. The weight of sadness colors every aspect of my existence: regret, loneliness, difficulty functioning. Much like my grandfather in that nursing home, I find myself navigating the solitude of my emotions.

Why am I telling you this? You see, Charlie, your grandfather's name was Martin Lucki. You and I are both named after him. David Martin Corvi. Charles Martin Corvi.

As I reflect on my grandfather's strength and vulnerability, I understand that seeking support from friends, family, and those who have been my pillars in the past is not a sign of weakness but an acknowledgment of the strength required to weather this storm. Withdrawing from those who care only

Letter 13

intensifies the feelings of depression, a reminder that healing is often found in shared sorrows.

And so, as I tangle with this complex dance of grief, I hold onto your love and guidance. In the echoes of my grandfather's emotions, I find comfort in understanding that strength is not the absence of sadness but the courage to face it.

Wherever you are, know you are missed and loved more than words can express.

Love,
Dad

Charlie's great grandfather and namesake, Martin Lucki

Letter 14

We suffer more often in imagination than in reality.

—Seneca

September 6, 2022

Dear Charlie,

    Nestled beside the patio behind our home, hang the Charlie Chimes—a thoughtful gift from close friends, arriving in the wake of your funeral. Suspended about four feet above the ground, they dance from an iron stand I carefully anchored into one of our mulch beds. Positioned gracefully next to a stone bench and our assortment of peonies and echinacea, these chimes compose a delicate tribute. Five 2-inch diameter silver tubes emit a peaceful melody, guided by a wooden striker suspended on a thin black line. Beneath the chimes, a silver sail bears the inscription "Heavenly Bells," and as the wind caresses them, they resonate with a deep, hollow beauty. The origins of wind chimes can be traced back to Ancient Rome and Eastern Asia, where they were crafted to dispel malevolent spirits and welcome benevolence.

Exactly one month has passed since my last letter. The end of summer swept by, a whirlwind of busyness and haste. Another season has come and gone, marked by significant milestones. William started first grade, while Alexander stepped into the world of preschool. I found myself coaching soccer, embracing the spirited chaos of the field. Work took me to Boston once this academic year, a reminder of the swift passage of time. Meanwhile, your mother, now 25 weeks pregnant, carries the promise of a new beginning.

In this time frame, Aunt Drea and Uncle Ernie welcomed Agnes Marie into the world, and Grandpap and Grandma celebrated their 43rd wedding anniversary. Time moves relentlessly forward in a continuous stream of moments. Yet, in this flow, you remain frozen—forever one day old, eternally six pounds, 15 ounces. The hope for the future nudges me to acknowledge this new reality, to understand the permanence of your absence, and to navigate the intricate dance of life with a heart that bears the weight of timeless love and loss.

Long days, fast years—the paradox of time echoes in these familiar phrases: "Don't blink," "It goes so fast," "Time flies," and "Time waits for no one."

Around the age of 27, amid the journey of self-discovery as an adult, engaged to your mother, and navigating the early years of my career, time revealed its elusive nature. Moments slipped through my fingers, leaving fragments of memories behind. Whole conversations unfolded, only to dissipate into the void of forgetfulness. The morning commute became a blur, a disconnection from the minutes that passed. Chapters of books and articles slipped through my grasp, their contents lost in the recesses of my mind. During conversations, I would find myself mentally absent, transported to another world, another life. Even in the pursuit of daily tasks, I would sit staring at my work, minutes slipping away without tangible accomplishments.

Letter 14

Your amazing mother was the first to notice the subtle shifts in my demeanor. She observed the vacant stare, the gaze that wandered into distant thoughts, and the lack of productivity that shadowed my days. Concerned, she became my anchor in seeking help. After consulting medical professionals and embarking on therapy with a psychologist, a revelation unfolded—a diagnosis of a form of Obsessive Compulsive Disorder (OCD).

The symptoms manifested as ruminations of the mind, also known as magical or fantasy thinking. In the labyrinth of my thoughts, I would construct intricate scenarios, replaying them endlessly. A missed opportunity became a fixation, prompting me to recreate the ideal outcome in my mind. Time was consumed organizing papers, files, or my schedule, yet the completion of actual work eluded me. These challenges unfolded amid everyday interactions with people. It became clear that my struggle to remember conversations and events was rooted in my absence—mentally transported to the recesses of my own mind, detached from the present moment.

Throughout several years of therapy and medication, I embarked on a journey to unravel the intricacies of my ruminating thoughts. Learning a myriad of mindfulness activities became my compass, guiding my wandering mind to stay anchored and present in daily life. Even now, more than a decade later, I continue to hone these skills. Muscle relaxation techniques serve as a tool to draw my attention to stress residing in my body. Mindful eating transforms meals into moments of intention, with each inhale embracing the aroma, each chew savoring the taste on my tongue. In conversations, my gaze is intentional—fixed on people's eyes and lips, fostering connection. Frequent journaling, a ritual of freewriting thoughts, becomes a cathartic release, a method to externalize what lingers within. I strive for heightened awareness of my thoughts, especially those that carry emotional weight, acknowledging them and then deliberately refocusing my attention to the present moment. Mindful breathing, a ritual woven into my daily fabric, offers moments of calm. Seated comfortably, inhaling and exhaling, I acknowledge passing thoughts and redirect my focus to the rhythmic flow of air moving in and out of my mouth.

Little did I know, my journey through mindfulness would prepare me for losing you. This unraveling of time underscored the fragility of moments that grow more profound in the context of your absence. Every time I pass your pictures in our home, they become meaningful pauses. The images of you curled into your mom's arms after delivery, swaddled in a blanket, and cradled in my arms evoke a spectrum of emotions. If I find myself rushing through the day, your chimes intervene, their gentle sound compelling me to halt. They serve as a reminder to slow down, to revel in the moment—whether it's time with William and Alexander, a comforting hug from your mom, the warmth of sunshine, the cool passing of a fall breeze, the scent of crisp winter air, or the solace found in a hot cup of coffee. When solitude embraces me while working in the backyard, the chimes ring, and in that melody, I sense your presence. It becomes our time to spend together.

Thank you, Charlie. You've evolved into my most cherished tool for mindfulness, anchoring me in the present moments of life. Day by day, I start to understand your memory is not a tether to the past but a guiding light in the present.

Wherever you are and whatever you are doing, know your mother and I carry your love in our hearts. We love you and miss you more than words can convey.

Love,
Dad

Letter 14

Cardinal with Charlie's Chimes in our backyard,
the inspiration for his logo

Letter 15

I will turn their mourning into joy;
I will comfort them and give them gladness for sorrow.

—Jeremiah 31:13

September 25, 2022

Dear Charlie,

Do events unfold with purpose, guided by a predetermined script we follow along as life happens to us? Or is life a sequence of chance occurrences, coincidences shaped by cause and effect relationships? One event unfolds, prompting a choice. Another follows, leading to yet another choice. And so the cycle continues. The intricacies of fate and chance weave through the fabric of our lives, questioning the very nature of our journey.

About a month or so after you were born, your mother and I decided to have dinner at a restaurant, just the two of us. It marked our first genuine alone time since we lost you. We planned to attend a support group for grieving parents afterward.

Letter 15

Upon reaching the meeting room, we found it empty. We sat and waited, but no one arrived. Seeking guidance, we asked hospital staff about the support group, and their response was, "Maybe it's across the street." Walking across to the medical building, we encountered a locked door after hours. Desperate, we called our therapist, hoping she could help us locate the group. As it turned out, the meetings had transitioned to virtual sessions due to COVID, with no communication on the website. How was any newly grieving parent supposed to access this resource? On the drive home, after not attending the support group, your mom and I both started to cry. The weight of navigating our grief that evening overwhelmed us.

Here we were, two educated individuals with means and resources, privileged in many ways, yet struggling to access the medical system. We couldn't locate this group and receive the much-needed support in grieving for you. It raised challenging questions about families without such privilege—what do they do? How do they access the intricacies of our medical system? How do they manage the emotional and financial burdens? How do they navigate the profound pain and sorrow of losing a baby?

A few months later, I spent time with my cousin Jeff, who lives close to our home. His children are close friends with William and Alexander. In the midst of all their laughter and play, I can't help but imagine you right there with them, part of the joyous mix.

In the midst of our conversation, Jeff expressed a desire to create a lasting memory of you. He mentioned the Akron Marathon's relay option, allowing a team of five to divide the 26.2 miles into shorter sections and complete the race together. Viewing it as a meaningful way to stay in shape, remember you, and honor your memory, we embraced the idea. Uncle Ernie, Aunt Erica, and Jeff's brother, Jason, joined us, forming our five-person relay team.

Over the following months, I trained and improved my endurance, slowly building up to the total eight miles I would run between the fourth and fifth leg of the marathon. Running through the neighborhoods and parks in my town provided me with yet another opportunity to spend time with and parent you.

As I took on the fourth leg of the marathon relay alone, the rhythmic pounding of my footsteps echoed a mix of determination and remembrance. The path ahead unfolded beneath the beating sun and towering trees of the Cuyahoga River Valley, each step a testament to resilience and commitment. The camaraderie with fellow runners, all bound by the shared purpose of completing the marathon, fueled a collective energy that was both empowering and meaningful. The transition to the fifth leg, where I joined Erica, brought a sense of unity and shared strength. Together, we approached the finish line, crossing it side by side as a symbol of our familial bond and the shared purpose behind Charlie's Challenge.

The relevance of our journey caught the attention of a local TV station, who were drawn to the distinctive blue Charlie's Challenge 2022 t-shirts we proudly wore. The interview captured not just the physical feat but also the profound significance of the event, reflecting the palpable energy and excitement that radiated from both the marathon runners and the spirited spectators along the way.

And so began Charlie's Challenge—our annual fundraiser and remembrance event dedicated to all that you are. Each year, we will undertake a different challenge in your memory. Charlie's Challenge stands as our main event, driving a fund we established in your name—The Charles Martin Corvi Fund.

Through our deeply tragic and emotional journey of losing you, we found solace in the embrace of excellent medical care and a network of support from family, friends, neighbors, colleagues, and clergy, who have continued to stand by us.

Letter 15

I continue to come to terms with your untimely departure, acknowledging the profound impact on our family.

Reflecting on that evening, we tried to go to the support group; your mother and I couldn't escape the thought of families and single parents who lack access to the resources needed to navigate the tragic loss of a baby. Guided by the acknowledgment of our own grief and with the support of Erica, your Godmother, we resolved that contributions to your fund would be a lifeline for those in need. The fund will collaborate with healthcare systems and non-profit organizations, supporting families grappling with financial or access burdens. Over time, the Charles Martin Corvi Fund aims to raise awareness about infant loss, advocate for enhanced support services, and contribute to research for prevention.

Did these two events unfold for a reason? Was our challenging experience that evening and the subsequent conversation with Jeff part of a greater design, or are they coincidences converging? I find myself contemplating whether you, in some way, have a hand in orchestrating these moments.

Your impact on this world, Charlie, goes beyond what we could have imagined. Through Charlie's Challenge and the Charles Martin Corvi Fund, your legacy continues to make a difference.

Wherever you are and whatever you are doing, know you are loved and missed more than anything.

Love,
Dad

Dear Charlie...Letters To My Son

Inaugural Charlie's Challenge 2022, Akron Marathon Relay
L-to-R: Jeff, Jason, Ernie, Erica, David

Charlie's Challenge 2022

Letter 15

Charlie's Aunt Erica crossing the finish line with me

Charlie's Challenge 2023

Letter 16

*The reality is that you will grieve forever.
You will not 'get over' the loss of a loved one;
you will learn to live with it.*

—Elisabeth Kübler-Ross

October 26, 2022

Happy Birthday, Charlie.

One year has slipped away since the last time we gazed upon you. A year—an inexplicable passage of time, a mindfuck of emotions. It marks 365 days since our arms held you. I've spent the last few days with little more than you on my mind. Your mother shares the same contemplation. Yesterday, an eerie feeling enveloped us both as we woke with the shared realization: one year ago, your tiny heart ceased its rhythmic beat. That was the day you left us. Mom recalled it as the final day she felt your gentle kicks. Did that last kick seal your umbilical cord's fate?

The same unanswered questions persist, echoing the day we lost you. We find ourselves retracing those painful steps together, moments etched in our hearts: the last time we felt

Letter 16

you, the ride to the hospital, the image of your still heart, mom enduring an epidural, the agonizing wait, and the haunting silence of the hospital room. We held you, but we had to return home without you, breaking the news to your brothers and facing a night without your comforting presence.

Your mom organized a thoughtful birthday celebration for you today centered around family activities. We planted 20 new daffodil bulbs in your garden, creating a living tribute. The boys eagerly unwrapped your presents, revealing a new board game we played together. Wooden pumpkins and a leaf became a collective painting project destined to decorate our house each fall. As a tradition, I've been crafting birthday videos for Alexander and William, capturing their growth each year with clips set to different songs. This year, I made one for you, featuring the heartfelt melody of "Bluebird" by Casen Watson, performed and recorded by a close friend. The video began with images of mom pregnant with you, followed by moments on the day you were born and at your funeral. It continued with various clips and photographs from events held in your honor this past year.

Collaborating with my cousin and your two aunts, we launched a website dedicated to your fund. An email was sent to the 200+ individuals who generously contributed their money, time, and love throughout the past year, sharing the news of the launch and the surpassing of the funding goal. Your impact is profound, offering support to those who have also experienced pregnancy or infant loss.

To mark your birthday, we ordered a chocolate cake with buttercream icing. We captured a heartfelt moment on video as the four of us sang happy birthday to you. William and Alexander took turns blowing out the solitary candle, a symbolic act for the day that should have been yours to celebrate.

This is agonizing.

Today should be filled with your laughter, tearing open presents, and indulging in your first birthday cake—embracing the pure childhood joy of celebrating. You should be nestled in the room next door, peacefully sleeping like your two brothers, wrapped in the safety and security of our home. Instead, here I am, pouring out my emotions in this letter. My frustration and anger intensify.

The week you died, your mother and I shared coffee with a couple who endured the loss of their firstborn to stillbirth. Their son's umbilical cord was wrapped around his neck, mirroring our own pain. I vividly recall the father's raw emotion and unbridled anger as we sat in that local coffee shop, sharing our stories. He spoke about a hole he punched in the wall—an unresolved mark of the pain he carried. It's been 18 years since their son's passing, and yet, the anger and the hole in the wall remain, a testament to the enduring impact of such a profound loss.

As I sit here in the quiet of my bedroom, I find myself awake, counting the minutes until the weight of your birthday lifts. My attempts to capture the whirlwind of emotions and thoughts for you are met with struggle. Downstairs, your ashes rest in their urn on the mantle, a tangible reminder of your absence. Despite the passing of a year, the anger and sadness linger, refusing to yield to the passage of time. Our family bears the weight of these emotions, crashing over us unexpectedly, a relentless force that feels profoundly unfair.

Navigating each day, I strive to hold it together for your mom and brothers, yet the ache persists. In your honor, we've opened a fund in your name and lighted candles in your memory. I am crafting a cedar chest to safeguard your possessions. Your brothers speak of you daily, the flowers in your garden continue to bloom, and our Charlie Chimes echo endlessly for you. Your presence is woven into our daily lives through scattered pictures around the house. We attend events to parent, cherish, and remember you. But amid these efforts, a lingering question remains:

Is it enough?

Letter 16

It's after midnight. Your birthday is now over and belongs to the past, marking a bitter milestone of one year without you. Charlie, I miss you deeply. Thank you for the everlasting mark you've left on our lives.

Love,
Dad

Charlie's Chest under construction

Letter 16

Charlie's Chest under construction

Katherine pregnant with Louis folding Charlie's clothes

Letter 17

And give glad tidings to those who patiently persevere.

—Quran 2:155

December 6, 2022

Dear Charlie,
    I want to let you know your little brother, Louis, was born last night. We are all so relieved and excited he's alive. This pregnancy has been different and more difficult than we could have imagined.
    Thank you, Charlie. Thank you for making the ultimate sacrifice so your younger brother can be here with us. Thank you for giving us another chance at holding one more baby. Thank you for safely watching over him and delivering him to us.
    We miss you terribly.

Love,
Dad

Letter 17

William with me

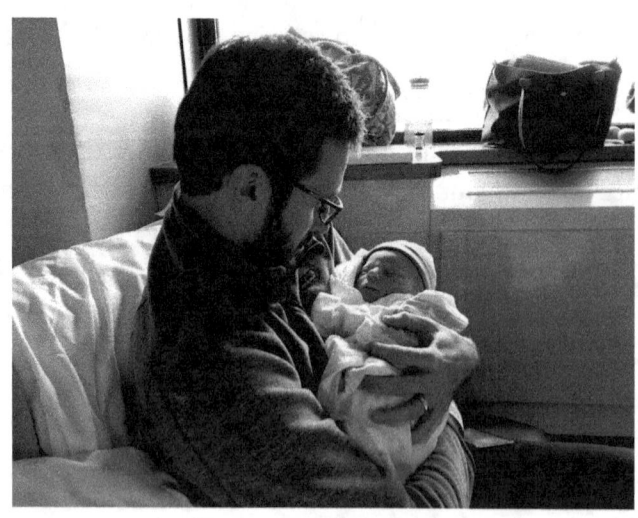

Alexander with me

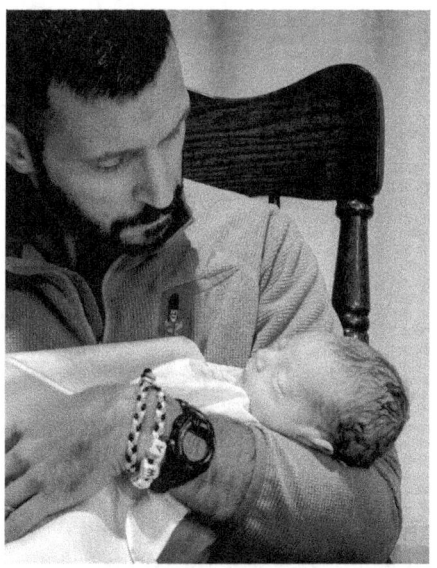

Charlie with me, Now I Lay Me Down To Sleep,
Marti Wagner

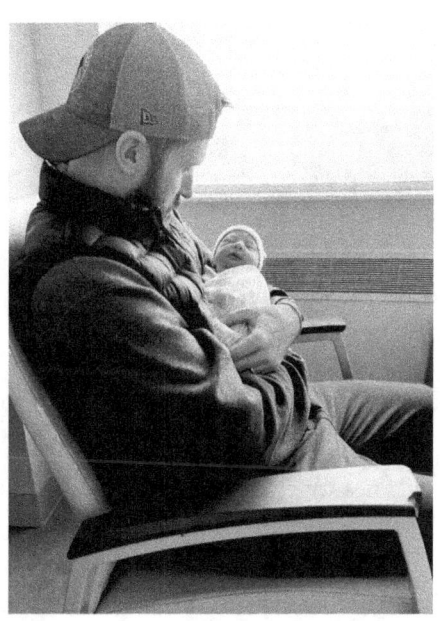

Louis with me

Letter 18

> We bereaved are not alone. We belong to the largest company in all the world—the company of those who have known suffering.
>
> —Helen Keller

May 27, 2024

Dear Reader,

Since Charlie's passing, I've come to realize the complexity of truths—how two seemingly contradictory realities can coexist. Life, as it unfolds, reveals few certainties. We human beings are intricate and multifaceted.

> Mourning for the departed can coexist with a sense of relief, knowing they are free from suffering.

> Anticipation for a much-needed vacation can be coupled with anxiety about the workload left behind.

> The drive and motivation in one's career can be shadowed by the guilt of neglecting personal balance.

Even in the unconditional love for our children, moments of frustration arise from their behaviors and decisions.

As another year passes, the paradox remains: Charlie is nowhere, and he is everywhere.
Across the great religions of the world, a shared recognition of the profound emotions and weight that accompany the journey of parenthood.

The prophet Muhammad (peace be upon him), is attributed as saying, "Paradise lies under the feet of your mother."

Judaism teaches, "Hear, my son, your father's instruction, and forsake not your mother's teaching, for they are a graceful garland for your head and pendants for your neck." —Proverbs 1:8-9

The Dalai Lama is quoted as saying, "Children need not only material support but also the support of compassionate and caring parents."

In the New Testament of the Holy Bible: "For God so loved the world, that he gave his only Son, that whoever believes in him should not perish but have eternal life." —John 3:16

In our role as parents, we impart numerous lessons to our children—tying shoelaces, riding bikes, throwing balls, braiding hair, cultivating kindness, and fostering friendships. Yet, amidst this, we sometimes overlook the profound lessons our children leave with us. It's now been almost three years since Charlie died. During this time, his absence has become a source of sincere education, unraveling lessons in grief, sorrow, love, healing, and joy. Here is a glimpse of the specific insights he has bestowed upon us:

Letter 18

- In our daily lives, we encourage each other not to shy away from speaking Charlie's name. Every day is touched by thoughts of him. Conversations are woven with mentions of him, letters are signed with his name, and a constant dialogue is maintained. Even at school, William and Alexander share his memory openly, discussing Charlie with classmates, divulging his story to friends and even strangers. In their creative expressions, they draw vivid pictures and immortalize Charlie in their words and images.

- Charlie is our guide in the way of communication, emphasizing the significance of open dialogue. We've learned to express our needs and boundaries, to articulate what is essential and what is not. Within our family, the words "We miss you, Charlie" are spoken openly, a shared acknowledgment of the void he's left. William and Alexander, too, are not hesitant to vocalize their longing for him. In moments of heightened emotions or challenges, they coined the term "Charlie Day" or "Charlie Moment" to acknowledge their continued grief. For me, particularly, the lessons run deeper. Charlie has been a catalyst for increasing tears, fostering vulnerability, and refining the art of listening.

- At 18 months old now, Louis even recognizes Charlie in pictures and says his name. He is our Rainbow Baby, and for those of you contemplating trying for another child after a loss, it is a unique decision for each family. I constantly tell Louis we are so happy he is here. We point to Charlie's picture and say his name. We never want Louis to feel like he is overshadowed by the loss of Charlie. We want his grief for the loss of his big brother to be immediate and not delayed.

- We can still parent Charlie. Like the pride we feel for our living boys when they overcome a feat, persevere through a challenge, or master a new skill, so, too, do we feel pride in all Charlie has accomplished. We parent Charlie by talking to him, by celebrating his birthday, by managing his fund, and by completing another Charlie's Challenge walk, run, or ride. Charlie has forever made a difference in our lives and the lives of many others.

- Charlie's teachings extend to the deep understanding that grief knows no bounds. It washes over our family like the rhythmic ebb and flow of the tide—relentless, perpetual. Initially, it crashed down with every waking second, the weight of loss imprinted in images like his motionless tiny body on the hospital scale. For me, those images lingered as the first and last sights of each day. Yet, the truest anguish lies in witnessing the immense journey Charlie's mother experienced to bring him to us and the ongoing struggle she battles in her role as his mother. Our living boys continue to navigate their unique trajectories of grief, each phase unveiling its challenges. As they mature, they will encounter new dimensions of grief, a continuous evolution in their understanding of loss.

- Charlie's final lesson is in the art of remembrance and healing. The impact of his fund, earnest and far-reaching, extends to countless lives he will never know. In our home, his memory is etched through the display of his pictures, a daily reminder of the love that endures. Daffodils bloom each year in his garden in our yard, a living tribute to his spirit. At Christmas, his stocking is hung, and at Easter, his basket is set out, so he is included in the holiday festivities. His birthday becomes a celebration, a commemoration of the life that almost was. The appearance of a cardinal, often seen to represent a loved one who has passed away, becomes a tender connection, a symbol of his enduring presence. And in the stories of other families grappling with loss,

Letter 18

Charlie lives on in the empathy and understanding extended to those who share a similar journey. Every mention, every gesture, is a testament to the unwavering remembrance of a beloved son.

If you are a parent who lost a child, no matter the age, but especially if that loss occurred during pregnancy or when your child was an infant, know you are not alone in your journey of loss, grief, and remembrance.

David

Candle with Charlie's Picture

Place setting for Charlie, December 2021

Recommended Readings

Bearing the Unbearable: Love, Loss, and the Heartbreaking Path of Grief by Joanne Cacciatore and Jeffrey Rubin

Even Now I Know by Michael Bullock

Forever Connected by Jessica Correnti

Jesus Calling by Sarah Young

Meditations by Marcus Aurelius

The Art of Losing: Poems of Grief and Healing by Kevin Young

The Christmas Box by Richard Paul Evans

Unexpecting: Real Talk on Pregnancy Loss by Rachel Lewis

Resources

The Charles Martin Corvi Fund partners with organizations that support families who have experienced pregnancy or infant loss.

Advocacy   Research   Grief   Remembrance

DONATE   **LEARN MORE**

SUPPORT FOR YOUR
GRIEVING CHILDREN

Kids Grief Support is a child life private practice that provides emotional and psychological support for children grieving after a death, trauma, move, transition, or other grief scenario. Available for support worldwide.

IN PERSON AND VIRTUAL SERVICES

Parent/Caregiver consultation sessions

Child/Teen therapeutic sessions are available to have hands-on, interactive, developmentally appropriate and individualized interventions to help children with understanding, processing, expressing, and healing through grief.

8600 Lasalle Rd Suite #636
Towson, MD 21286

 contact@kidsgriefsupport.com

 @kidsgriefsupport

www.kidsgriefsupport.com

Maryland Lighthouse Chapter

of

Reflections Grief and Wellness Care

Illuminating the path of
HOPE & HEALING
after loss

marylandlighthouse@reflectionsgwc.org

www.reflectionsgwc.org

Christmas Box Angel of Hope
Children's Memorial

Due to the incredible passion and work of a group of dedicated bereaved parents, the Angel was brought to Stow, Ohio in 2001. The Christmas Box Angel of Hope Children's Memorial is a peaceful place for grieving parents whose children have died, before or after birth, to mourn, heal, and remember their beloved children. It has also given parents, family, and friends an opportunity to connect with one another and share their grief as they visit the memorial.

HEALTHYbirthDAY  Creator of

A Leader in Stillbirth Prevention

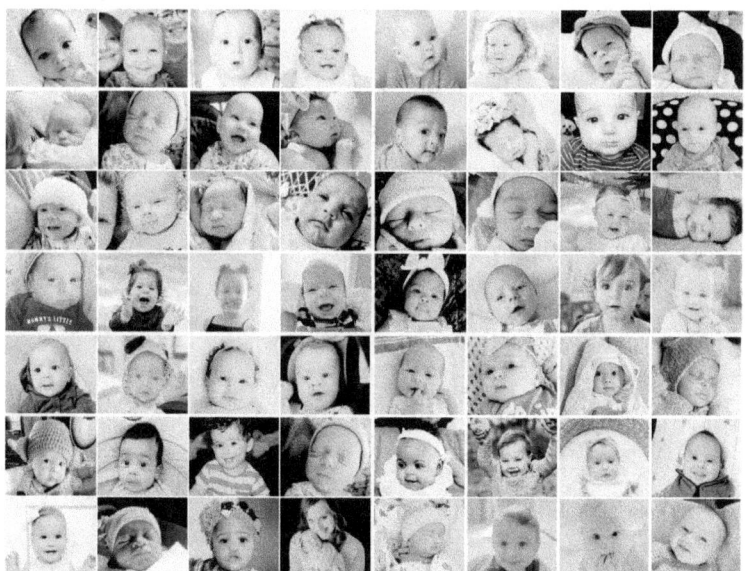

OUR MISSION

Healthy Birth Day, Inc. is a 501(c)(3) nonprofit organization dedicated to the prevention of stillbirth through programming, advocacy, and research. We help save babies using the evidence-based *Count the Kicks* stillbirth prevention program, which educates expectant parents on the importance of tracking their babies' movements in the third trimester of pregnancy and empowers them to speak up if they notice a change.

OUR VISION

Our vision is to replicate the success of the highly effective *Count the Kicks* program in all 50 states. We hope to reduce America's stillbirth rate by 32% as we have done in Iowa, which would save 7,500 babies from preventable stillbirth every year.

CONTACT US

Healthy Birth Day, Inc.
515-650-8685
info@healthybirthday.org

HealthyBirthDay.org | CountTheKicks.org

3 WAYS TO GET INVOLVED

1. **Order *Count the Kicks* educational materials.** They are FREE in nearly 30 states, and available for a low cost in all other states. Find them at CountTheKicks.org.

2. **Share the *Count the Kicks* app!** Tell every expectant parent you know to download *Count the Kicks* and use it every day starting at 28 weeks.

3. **Advocate for stillbirth prevention!** We are advocating for stillbirth prevention legislation in Congress that will help to address the stillbirth crisis by supporting research and prevention efforts. We encourage you to learn more and show your support at bit.ly/StopStillbirth.

Contact us today to schedule a free assessment.

Your mental health is our priority.

216-308-7592
ownbbc@birthingbeautiful.org

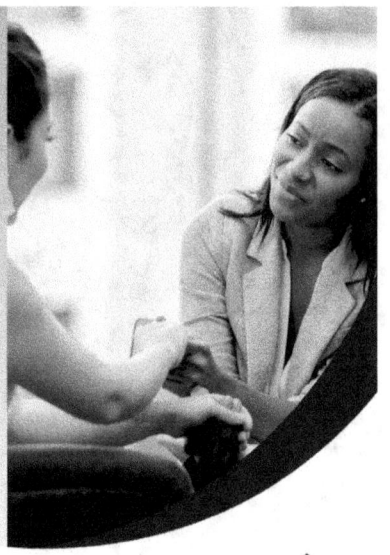

www.birthingbeautiful.org

Mission Statement:

SAD DADS CLUB helps fellow bereaved fathers navigate life after loss by nurturing a supportive community and providing access to mental health services.

Virtual Engagement:

- Weekly **Zoom (Thursdays, 8:30pm ET)** where dads share their struggles, successes, and stories. Registration: saddadsclub.com/events

- Private **SDC Discord** channel active 24/7.

In-Person Engagement:

- Weekend retreats, sports outings, brewery meet-ups, hikes, and more.

- In-person gatherings updated regularly on our website.

Benefits:

SDC community members have experienced:
- Better sleep.
- Increased focus at work.
- More present with their partner and living child(ren).

www.saddadsclub.com // @sad.dads.club // info@saddadsclub.com

Back In His Arms Again

Believing that every life is precious and deserving of respect, Back In His Arms Again honors life from conception until death.

We are a charitable organization of collaborative resources providing education, care, guidance and financial services for families in need who are experiencing the loss of a child as well as those providing care.

Services Offered

Guidance for navigating the burial or cremation process
Emotional support through the grieving process
Peer-to-peer support group
Provide gowns, layettes, blankets, prayer shawls
Financial assistance for burial if needed

Contact Us

www.backinhisarmsagain.com
614-906-3115
Kambra Conley, *Foundress, Executive Director*
kambra@backinhisarmsagain.com
Amy Tatz, *President*
Amy@backinhisarmsagain.com

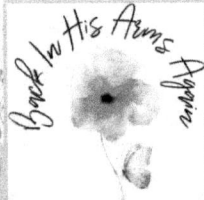

Because Every Life Matters

Enhancing Awareness, Providing Resources, and Supporting Families Experiencing Pregnancy and Infant Loss!

Find us at: www.milesmission.com

Follow us on Facebook, Instagram, or LinkedIn

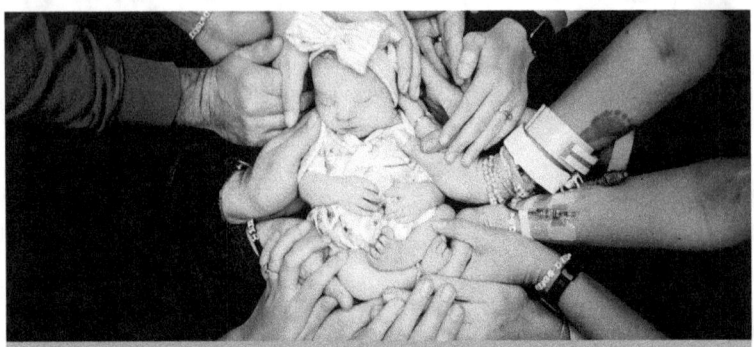

nilmdts
Now I Lay Me Down to Sleep

Our Mission

To introduce remembrance photography to parents experiencing the loss of a baby with a free gift of professional portraiture.

Our Reach

NILMDTS has gifted more than 70,000 complimentary portrait sessions since 2005.

Our Work

- Free sessions for families
- Remembrance events
- Free digital retouch services
- Medical Affiliate Program

Get Involved

- Affiliated Photographer
- Digital Retouch Artist
- Medical Affiliate
- Dispatcher

Connect with Us

 headquarters@nilmdts.org

 nowilaymedowntosleep.org

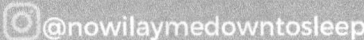 @nowilaymedowntosleep

www.ingramcontent.com/pod-product-compliance
Lightning Source LLC
Chambersburg PA
CBHW052146070526
44585CB00017B/1997